OUR SAVIOR FROM SELF-DOUBT

OUR SAVIOR FROM SELF-DOUBT

GAYLAMARIE ROSENBERG

Published by the Religious Studies Center, Brigham Young University, Provo, Utah, in cooperation with Deseret Book Company, Salt Lake City.
Visit us at rsc.byu.edu.

Printed in the United States of America by Sheridan Books, Inc.

Deseret Book is a registered trademark of Deseret Book Company.
Visit us at DeseretBook.com.

Cover design and interior layout by Emily V. Rogers.

Library of Congress Cataloging-in-Publication Data

Names: Rosenberg, Gaylamarie, 1963- author.
Title: Our Savior from self-doubt / Gaylamarie Rosenberg.
Description: Provo, Utah : Religious Studies Center, Brigham Young University ; Salt Lake City, Utah : Deseret Book, [2022] | Includes index. | Summary: "Self-doubt limits our perception of our potential and diminishes our joy and hope in who we are and what we can become. When we don't feel good about ourselves, we have help. Jesus Christ saves us not only from our imperfections but also from our imperfect understanding of ourselves. This book explores sources of self-doubt and the impact of positive psychology in changing our thought patterns. It emphasizes an often-ignored dimension of the Atonement of Jesus Christ: how Christ helps us overcome self-doubt and unproductive thinking"-- Provided by publisher.
Identifiers: LCCN 2021044373 | ISBN 9781950304257 (hardback)
Subjects: LCSH: Jesus Christ--Mormon interpretations. | Self-perception--Religious aspects--Church of Jesus Christ of Latter-day Saints. | Self-perception--Religious aspects--Mormon Church. | Self-doubt. | Self-esteem--Religious aspects--Church of Jesus Christ of Latter-day Saints. | Self-esteem--Religious aspects--Mormon Church. | Christian life--Mormon authors.
Classification: LCC BX8656 .R67 2022 | DDC 248.4/89332--dc23/eng/20220208
LC record available at https://lccn.loc.gov/2021044373

CONTENTS

ACKNOWLEDGMENTS

I am indebted to many friends and colleagues for making this book possible. First, I want to thank Ana De Agostini. While we were serving on the BYU Women's Conference Committee, she encouraged me to write a book—the starting point of this journey for me. I appreciate her belief that I could tackle such a task.

I'm grateful to Denys Snyder for her writing expertise. Her helpful writing suggestions early in this process were a tremendous help in finding my own voice. I'm indebted to Stephanie Sorensen for poring over early drafts with me to sift through what was worth saying. And thanks to Kim Sandoval from the BYU Faculty Publishing Service for making this a better book.

My heartfelt appreciation goes to Maylarie Ostler, my twin sister, for her encouraging and candid suggestions that made this book more real and relatable for all; Caroline Kreutzkamp for her unfailing friendship and support in this project; Sarah Bodine and Lynne Thorley for their suggestions and continued support in my writing and speaking assignments; Peggy Worthen for listening and for offering words of encouragement these past few years; and Fiona Givens for believing in me and my work—her gracious words answered prayers.

In addition, I gratefully acknowledge many friends and family members that have read drafts, offered suggestions, listened to excerpts, shared stories, and given me encouragement. They have all inspired me with stories and examples of how Christ's goodness and grace saves us from doubt and despair. I'm a better person because of their light and love.

I express my deep appreciation to those at the Religious Studies Center at Brigham Young University. Thank you to Scott C. Esplin, who encouraged me to submit my manuscript to the RSC; Julie Newman for her editing expertise and her careful and thoughtful suggestions; Emily V. Rogers for her work on the cover and text design; R. Devan Jensen for his valuable suggestions and encouragement; and Brock Dowdle for help in sharing my message. Additionally, I am sincerely grateful to publications director Jared W. Ludlow, publications coordinator Joany O. Pinegar, production supervisor Brent R. Nordgren, and student editing interns Myla Parke, Mikaela Wilkins, and Abby Knudsen.

Last, I thank my family for their unwavering support: Karen Marie for spending hours lying on the floor in the study, listening to the latest draft of a chapter and giving wonderful suggestions; Eliza for her continued encouragement and enthusiasm; and most importantly, my husband, John, for walking this writing journey with me and encouraging me through every step. His unfailing support kept me going. So many of the ideas and concepts presented are ideas I have learned from him and with him. I can't count how many times he has read through each chapter and given me valuable editing and content suggestions. When I had self-doubt about my ability to complete this project, he would say, "Why don't you read your own book!" The great irony in writing this book has been to battle my own doubt that I could do it. I'm profoundly grateful to my Savior for joining me on this adventure. He helped me to focus on what I could do—with Him. Because of Him, I was able to dig deep into spiritual reservoirs that helped me transfer what was in my heart to words on a page.

INTRODUCTION

A few years ago, my husband and I had the unique experience of walking the Camino de Santiago (the "Way of Saint James") in northern Spain with students from Brigham Young University (BYU). The Camino de Santiago pilgrimage was established over one thousand years ago to honor the Apostle James for his ministry in Spain. Much like pioneer treks that members of The Church of Jesus Christ of Latter-day Saints participate in today to pay tribute to their pioneer roots, the Camino celebrates Christian roots in Europe. Many people walk its paths in honor of Christ, celebrating how Christ has helped them or seeking His help and healing.

The Camino route winds through rolling green hills, sparkling streams, beautiful wildflowers, charming medieval churches, and quaint towns with lots of cows. While walking the path, you frequently see people from other countries who greet you by saying, "*Buen camino*" ("Have a nice journey"). They carry a scallop shell—a symbol that they are a *peregrino* ("pilgrim") making the trek to the city of Santiago. The most traditional route, called the French Road, is five hundred miles long. In 2019, 347,578 people from 187 countries walked some or all

Photos taken on the Camino de Santiago that show the landscape of the trek. Photos by author.

of the Camino path—a path that was created to celebrate the impact of Christ on our mortal journeys.[1]

My favorite part of walking the Camino de Santiago was watching people make spiritual connections. One father brought his intellectually gifted son to *disconnect* him from his computer and help him value *connecting* with God and others. Another person walked the path to heal from the insecurity and bitterness resulting from two abusive marriages. Her goal was to open her heart to Christ and seek His healing power as she walked.

I was particularly intrigued by a conversation I had on the Camino with a college student. She struggled with doubt about herself and her connection to God. She told me she wanted to know if God loved her and cared about her. Thoughtfully, she asked, "Does He believe in me? With all the people in the world, is there really a God in heaven who knows *me* personally?" Was the Savior there for her? Did she need to go it alone and rely on her own ability, or could she trust that there was a God in heaven who would help her? My heart was filled with love for her. I wanted to do all I could to witness of a Savior who knew her personally, who did not doubt her ability to progress, and who could help her through any struggle with self-doubt.

In the last few years of teaching college students, I have noticed their increasing struggles with doubt—doubt about God and doubt about themselves. My greatest concern is that many of them try to overcome these feelings alone, without the help of our Savior. Without His strength to guide them, they might see self-doubt settle in and paralyze their efforts to move forward.

The Paralyzing Impact of Self-Doubt

Doubting that we have what it takes to succeed is common. We doubt we have ability, talent, or motivation. "I can't do it," we say. "I'm not as capable as others." "I'm not anyone special, and I'm too overwhelmed to do it all." "I'm not perfect and never will be." I relate to a bumper sticker that says, "God put me on this earth to accomplish a certain number of things. Right now I am so far behind that I will never die."[2] If you feel your weaknesses are overwhelming, you are not alone. We all have imperfections. No one is exempt. And none of us likes having them!

It is likely that someone close to you is struggling with self-doubt. You may have coworkers who doubt the value of their contributions, a spouse who is unhappy with his or her appearance, children who feel untalented compared to their peers, friends who doubt that they are worthy of God's help, or members in your ward who feel inadequate to serve. The possibilities are endless.

Elder Jeffrey R. Holland spoke of self-doubt in a BYU devotional: "[Self-doubt] can have damaging effects that block our growth, dampen our spirit, diminish our hope, and leave us vulnerable to other more conspicuous evils. . . . I know of nothing Satan uses quite so cunningly or cleverly in his work."[3] Satan aims to destroy our sense of identity. He will do all he can to prevent us from accepting who we are and what we can become. While serving as a counselor in the Relief Society General Presidency, Sheri L. Dew said, "The Lord's motives stand in stark contrast to those of Lucifer, who is obsessed with attempting to make us feel less than who we are as sons and daughters of God."[4] Satan's work could be described with some *d* words: discouragement, distraction, disconnection, deceit, and doubt. No wonder he is called the devil and desires to damn the souls of God's children. He seeks to *disable* our efforts, but Christ seeks to *enable* our progression. There are several *e* words that reflect the Savior's efforts: encourage, empower, enhance, elevate, edify, expiate, educate, and enlighten. No wonder He desires to endow us with eternal life and exaltation.

With our understanding of God's plan of salvation, we know who we are and what we may become. We know we are born in God's image and endowed with divine potential. We know Jesus Christ came to save us from anything that would limit our ability to become like Him. We know He lives, loves us, is mindful of us, strengthens us, and has the power to make all things possible. So why do we doubt ourselves? What holds us back?

We doubt ourselves for several reasons. We become impatient with our progress. We dwell on weaknesses, making us more critical and judgmental of ourselves. We fear we are not enough. We compare our weaknesses to others' strengths. We try to do too many things at once. We feel unworthy of God's help and rely on our own strength.

Fortunately, self-doubt can motivate us to seek divine refinement. Imperfections don't need to be debilitating; they are an opportunity for growth. Having imperfections was one of the conditions of mortality that we as premortal spirits joyfully embraced. Having a realistic view of our abilities produces humility, which is powerful in progression—it opens our hearts to the Spirit and to divine tutoring. On the other hand, if we don't accept Christ's help, self-doubt can paralyze our efforts to develop our potential.

Changing Our Focus

I had a memorable experience at a parent-teacher conference when my daughter was in fourth grade. Her teacher explained how my daughter was doing and then remarked, "If I want my students to improve their writing skills, I point out the good things they are doing. This approach motivates them to improve." Then he looked at me and said, "Just remember, whatever you focus on will increase."

I nodded and replied, "Nice tip."

He then spoke about my daughter's social skills and said again, "Whatever behavior you focus on will increase. If you focus on the negative, the negative will increase. If you focus on the positive, the positive will increase." As I was leaving, he reiterated, "You know, the one thing I wish parents would remember about raising children is that whatever they focus on will increase."

I smiled. "I think I got it." And I haven't forgotten.

In my research about self-doubt, I've discovered many good ideas and skills for changing unproductive thinking. But none ring truer to me than the advice I received from my daughter's teacher: *whatever we focus on will increase.* When we focus on our weaknesses and inadequacies, those weaknesses and inadequacies will continue to occupy our thoughts. So if we feel that we are stuck in a rut of negative self-talk, we need a change of focus!

Clinical psychologists and therapists have found that people are significantly better at dealing with negative self-talk when they change their focus from *fixing* negative emotions to enhancing positive emotions. Here are a few examples:

- In his book *Flourish*, clinical psychologist Martin Seligman explains the impact of changing theories and techniques from "What is wrong here?" to "What is right here?" with positive psychology. This approach focuses on positive emotions, engagement, meaning, positive accomplishment, and good relationships. One of the simple yet powerful exercises he teaches is to write down daily "three things that went well today and why they went well." Changing the focus from negative emotions to positive emotions enables a person to flourish.[5]

- In *The Seven Principles for Making Marriage Work*, marriage therapist John Gottman explains, "I was not able to crack the code to saving marriages until I started to analyze what went *right* in happy marriages." He states that couples are "emotionally intelligent" when they spend more time enhancing their strengths rather than dwelling on their weaknesses.[6]
- In *Mindset: The New Psychology of Success*, psychologist Carol Dweck addresses how people cope with failure and perceive success. She studied how students grappled with hard problems and found that there are basically two mindsets: a fixed mindset or a growth mindset. Those students who believed in a growth mindset focused on challenges as stepping stones to progress and felt optimistic about their possibilities.[7]
- In *What Happy People Know*, behavioral therapist Dan Baker explains that "fear of not having enough" and "fear of not being enough" prevent us from progression. His antidote to this fear is appreciation—appreciation for what we have, what we can do, and what brings us joy. He helps clients focus on strengths to develop and blessings to enjoy.[8]
- In *The Gifts of Imperfection*, social worker Brené Brown explains how our imperfections often hold us back from finding happiness in the present moment. She focuses on teaching "wholehearted living" that emphasizes the gifts and blessings of learning through our imperfections.[9]

All these well-known writers and mental health experts have emphasized the powerful influence of retraining our minds to produce more positive, realistic, and helpful thoughts instead of negative and unhelpful ones. They have successfully helped others create mental resilience and strength by changing their focus to positive emotions—which results in more positive emotions. Training our minds to focus on positive thoughts and actions increases our self-motivation and discipline, augments our ability to think clearly and rationally, trains us to be more reflective than reactive, and reduces negative mental chatter: the self-talk that gets in our way of personal peace and progression.

My desire is to help readers challenge and change unproductive thoughts about themselves. We will discuss the source of doubt, and we will learn ways to increase our focus on healthy and productive thoughts that bring out the best in us by

- focusing on patient progress instead of immediate perfection,
- focusing on how God sees us instead of how we see ourselves,
- focusing on what we can do instead of what we can't do,
- focusing on developing our own abilities instead of comparing our abilities,
- focusing on doing one needful task at a time instead of several at a time,
- focusing on Christ's willingness to forgive instead of our unworthiness to be forgiven, and
- focusing on Christ's invitation to walk with Him instead of trying to walk alone.

Recognizing our thought patterns is a crucial step in overcoming self-doubt. I started writing in a journal a long time ago to help me identify healthy versus unhealthy thoughts. I gave my journal a title: "Think-in-Ink." If you are like me, writing down what you're thinking can bring clarity to your mind. At the end of each chapter of this book, there is an invitation to focus on productive thoughts and a "think-in-ink" challenge with space provided to write down your thoughts and ideas.

"All-One" versus "At-One"

Overcoming self-doubt requires a willingness to change our focus. Our ability to change our focus to positive, productive thoughts and actions is enhanced most powerfully when we seek and accept divine assistance. First and foremost, overcoming self-doubt requires a willingness to keep our focus on our Savior and Redeemer Jesus Christ. We speak often of the Atonement of Jesus Christ and His redeeming and enabling powers that help us overcome physical and spiritual death. But we may forget that He can also help us overcome feelings of self-doubt, insecurity, low self-esteem, and inadequacy, all of which obstruct the path that leads us to our divine potential.

There is a stark contrast between the words *alone* and *atone*. Both have the same root word: *one*. *Alone*, "all-one," means to be isolated, to have no help, or to have no one present. When we are alone, we depend on ourselves. In contrast, *atone*, "at-one," means to become united or reconciled.[10] Adam and Eve left Eden for the lone world—apparently a contrast to the divine society of paradise. But even in the lone world they were promised they would not be alone. The good news of the Atonement is that we are not alone. We have the Savior! He invites us to be united—"at-one"—with Him. Christ invites us into a perfectly unified relationship with Him and our Father: "That they may be one, even as we are one: I in them, and thou in me, that they may be made perfect in one" (John 17:22–23). This invitation to be united with Christ and our Father is an invitation to accept Their help in the refining process to become like Them. Christ will help us change the way we think, the way we feel, and our motivation to act. We progress with Him. We become our best selves with Him. We have hope and happiness because of Him.

We are not left alone when we don't feel good about ourselves. Christ invites us to walk with Him, so why should we try to deal with self-doubt alone? Instead, we can focus on the Savior's ability to help us. Sheri Dew asked, "Are we satisfied with far less than the Lord is willing to give us, essentially opting to go it alone here rather than partner with the Divine?"[11] We choose to receive His help and strength. "For I the Lord thy God will hold thy right hand, saying unto thee, Fear not; *I will help thee*" (Isaiah 41:13; italics added).

As we focus on the Savior's help in overcoming self-doubt—by focusing on His patience, charity, power, voice, forgiveness, and gifts to us—we will see the depth of His love and support for each one of us. With this new understanding, fear will give way to faith, doubt will change to diligence, and weakness will transform into strength. Peace, hope, confidence, and happiness will come into our lives as we embrace the Savior's ministering to each of us personally.

Farther and Higher with Christ

In a medieval book compiled about the Camino de Santiago, called the *Codex Calixtinus*, we find a Latin hymn dedicated to the Apostle James. It admonishes pilgrims to go "farther and higher with God's help."[12] As I walked the Camino last summer, I received a powerful reminder of the importance of accepting Christ's invitation to walk with Him and to trust in His ability to empower us with personal strength and confidence.

Enoch is a perfect example of going "farther and higher with Christ" when faced with feelings of self-doubt. In Moses 6, God asked Enoch to preach His word, to which Enoch replied, "Why is it that I have found favor in thy sight? . . . All the people hate me; for I am slow of speech" (verse 31). Enoch believed that God had chosen him, but he feared he was not eloquent enough to succeed in his calling. God asked Enoch to try and then promised, "Behold my Spirit is upon you, wherefore all thy words will I justify; and the mountains shall flee before you, and the rivers shall turn from their course; and thou shalt abide in me, and I in you; therefore walk with me" (verse 34).

How do we experience the Savior's help when we are faced with doubt about who we are and what we may become? What are signs of "abiding" in His presence? We help each other recognize the Savior's help by sharing about our faith in Him. Speaking of a friend who strengthened him, William E. Berrett, a former patriarch in the Church, remarked, "We could warm our hands by the fire of his faith."[13] I love that metaphor because it makes me imagine a long journey walking together with family and friends through life, with evening fires to warm our hands. On the Camino route I often saw our BYU students warming their hands by the fire of the faith of those around them. Likewise, the fire of these students' faith warmed the hands of many strangers they met from all over the world, who were also gathering to share how they experienced the warmth of our Savior. We need each other. We encourage each other to rely on divine insight. I'm thankful for the many family members and friends that have helped me challenge doubts about myself by sharing how they experience the warmth, love, and strength of Christ.

The purpose of this book is to boost confidence—confidence empowered by Christ. My desire is to increase awareness of several sources of self-doubt and to share ways we can move our focus from our weaknesses to the strength made possible through divine help. I have felt peace and joy in my life as I have taken my feelings of weakness and inadequacy to the Lord and felt His strength. I hope you will feel the warmth of the Savior as you read about His willingness to strengthen you. I know He believes in you. I know He believes in what you may become with His help.

Feelings of inadequacy must not prevent us from pressing forward; they are often the very means by which we open our hearts and seek the Savior's companionship. I invite you to consider what kind of impact self-doubt has had in your life and what you can do to accept the Savior's help. Doctrine and Covenants 62:1 reads, "Jesus Christ [is] your advocate, who knoweth the weakness of man and how to succor them." He is our Savior from self-doubt.

Notes

1. See "Informe estadístico: Año 2019," Oficina de Acogida al Peregrino, pp. 2, 4–8, http://oficinadelperegrino.com/wp-content/uploads/2016/02/peregrin aciones2019.pdf.
2. This saying is attributed to Bill Watterson. See Bill Watterson, "Bill Watterson Quotes," Brainy Quote, https://www.brainyquote.com/authors/bill-watterson -quotes.
3. Jeffrey R. Holland, "For Times of Trouble" (Brigham Young University devotional, March 18, 1980), 1, speeches.byu.edu.
4. Sheri L. Dew, "Our Only Chance," *Ensign*, May 1999, 66.
5. Martin E. P. Seligman, *Flourish: A Visionary New Understanding of Happiness and Well-Being* (New York: Simon and Schuster, 2011), 33, 70.
6. John M. Gottman, *The Seven Principles for Making Marriage Work* (New York: Three Rivers Press, 1999), 3, 46.
7. See Carol S. Dweck, *Mindset: The New Psychology of Success* (New York: Ballantine Books, 2016), 6–7.
8. Dan Baker and Cameron Stauth, *What Happy People Know: How the New Science of Happiness Can Change Your Life for the Better* (New York: St. Martin's Griffin, 2003), 78–81.
9. Brené Brown, *The Gifts of Imperfection: Let Go of Who You Think You're Supposed to Be and Embrace Who You Are* (Center City, MN: Hazelden, 2010), 1–6.
10. See *Merriam-Webster*, s.vv. "alone," "atone," https://www.merriam-webster.com /dictionary.
11. Sheri Dew, "We Are Not Alone," *Ensign*, November 1998, 95.
12. "Dum pater familias" (hymn), lines 19–20, in *Codex Calixtinus*, la.wikisource .org/wiki/codex_calixtinus/dum_pater_familias.
13. Quoted in Boyd K. Packer, "A Tribute to the Rank and File of the Church," *Ensign*, May 1980, 62.

chapter one

FOCUS ON HIS PATIENCE

Feelings of self-doubt come when we are impatient with ourselves. The Savior is patient with us and encourages us to focus on patient progress instead of immediate perfection. We can focus on who we are already instead of who we are not—yet. Instead of striving to have perfect abilities, we can focus on our perfectibility ("perfect-ability") with Christ.

Ten days after my husband and I were married, we left for Spain to direct a study abroad group in Madrid. I was excited to learn from him, since he was a professor of Spanish literature. We were both older when we met, and we felt fortunate to finally find each other. After meeting, we had a very short courtship and engagement before we married, so when we hurried off to Spain, we had not known each other for very long. I had just completed graduate work in family sciences and was determined to practice the skills and theories I had studied on my new husband. I had high expectations for our marriage. Since I was trained in marriage-relationship skills, I was confident our marriage would be perfect from day one!

After several weeks of running here and there with him, I felt a little neglected because his mind seemed to be preoccupied with his work. I looked at him one day and said, "Sometimes I feel like you love Spain more than me." With a smile, he responded, "Well, I've known Spain longer." He thought it was funny. After all, it was a silly question—of course he loved me more than he loved Spain. I was his bride, sealed to him for eternity! But I wasn't laughing. He saw the serious look on my face and said something like "Can we just *enjoy where and who we are* and not expect our marriage to be perfect—yet?" He was inviting me to be happy with our marriage so far and not to be discouraged with what we hadn't yet created. After all, we had been married for only one month! Could we just take one day at a time and enjoy our marriage for what it was at that stage? I was expecting to learn a lot about Spain from my husband, but that day I learned about patience, perfection, and the Creation process from him.

The Creation Process

God is a patient creator. Elder Richard L. Evans taught, "There seems to be little evidence that the Creator of the universe was ever in a hurry. Everywhere, on this bounteous and beautiful earth, and to the farthest reaches of the firmament, there is evidence of patient purpose and planning and working and waiting."[1] In Genesis 1 we read the account of the creation of the earth. Verse 10 ends the third day of creation with the phrase "And God saw that it was good." We learn the same thing about each subsequent day: each day was good. God was pleased with the state and progress of each day, content with what had been created thus far. He wasn't concerned that on day two He had not yet created beautiful flowers and trees. God was perfectly fine with not having animals on day four. My husband reminded me, "At the end of day five, God did not say, 'After all this work and all this time, all I have to show for my effort is fish.'"[2] Instead, after each day of creation, our biblical account says that God was pleased with the progress of that day and the progress toward day seven.

I believe our Heavenly Father views our process of becoming perfect the same way He viewed the process of the Creation: each individual day or stage is *good*—even the stages of imperfection. I believe He would say to us, "You are good! Look at your progress this day. Look how I have blessed you already." We can feel satisfaction in the progress we make each day, imperfect and messy as it may feel, and prepare ourselves for the next day. We should not think that God is disappointed with us until we reach restful day seven. We can recognize how God has helped us already. For each day is good—and necessary—in His eyes. (For previous thoughts shared on the Creation and the process of becoming, see notes 2 and 3.)[3]

God is pleased with each day of the creation of the earth, which helps us visualize His satisfaction with our daily efforts in the creation of a Christlike nature. Courtesy of Pixabay.

My husband's request that I "not expect our marriage to be perfect—yet" was an invitation to be patient. He invited me to see the goodness and growth in the present moment. Like the Creation process, I could see each day as good and necessary. I could be happy with my marriage and enjoy each day my husband and I had to grow together instead of expecting it to be perfect and complete already. My husband's comment gave me peace that he didn't expect me to be perfect in everything and reminded me to do the same for him. I realized that I could find hope and happiness—even with all our imperfections and inexperience—not only in our marriage but in our individual journeys.

You may find yourself, like me, frequently needing a reminder that God is patient with you and will never forsake you. Elder Marvin J. Ashton taught, "We do not have to worry about the patience of God, because he is the personification of patience, no matter where we have been, what we have done, or what we, to this moment, have allowed ourselves to think of ourselves."[4] What have we allowed? We may find ourselves thinking, "I'm not good enough." "I don't have what it takes." "I'm not perfect and never will be." We want drive-through progress: fast, easy, and inexpensive! But our pathway to perfection requires dining in: although expensive and time intensive, patience gives us time to plan, time to wait, and time to enjoy each other's company. Patience helps us see that the outcome is worth the wait.

Recognizing God's patience helps us overcome self-doubt by changing our focus to how He has helped us already and how He will continue to help us. God knows that for us to reach day seven—a state of perfection—we will have to be patient with ourselves and others.

Impatience Gets in the Way

Impatience gets in the way of progress. When we're impatient, we focus on who we are *not* instead of who God has helped us to become already. We expect immediate perfection. And then we miss the daily goodness and growth in front of us. We don't notice the husband who took the garbage out, because we wish he was reading to the kids. We don't acknowledge the daughter who just said thank you, because we want her to pick up her dirty clothes. We overlook the neighbor who raked our leaves, because we want him to cut down his tree that's scattering the leaves. We fail to appreciate a sibling's gesture to wish us a happy birthday, because she is ten days late.

In other words, we see what others lack instead of what they can offer. We don't cherish the moment, because it's not good enough—we want it to be better *now*! Impatience prevents us from seeing what we have done, because we are fixated on the *undone*. Impatience threatens our faith in God's eternal plan. Elder Neal A. Maxwell taught, "Patience is tied very closely to faith in our Heavenly Father. Actually, when we are unduly impatient we are suggesting that we know what is best—better than does God." He further explained that impatience is like constantly pulling up the daisies to see how the roots are doing or opening the oven door every five minutes to see if the cake is done baking. "Without patience we will learn less in life. We will see less; we will feel less; we will hear less. Ironically, 'rush' and 'more' usually mean 'less.'"[5]

When we try to rush our growth, we hinder our growth. We miss the opportunity to be tutored by God, and we create unrealistic expectations for ourselves—expectations not imposed on us by God.

Perfectionism versus *Perfectibility*

Elder Gerrit W. Gong taught that "our campfire of faith can encourage us to remember perfection is in Christ, not in ourselves or in the perfectionism of the world."[6] What is perfectionism? Psychologist Brené Brown describes perfectionism as "*a self-destructive and addictive belief system that fuels this primary thought:* If I look perfect, live perfectly, and do everything perfectly, I can avoid or minimize the painful feelings of shame, judgment, and blame." She further says that "*perfectionism is* not *self-improvement.* [It] is, at its core, about trying to earn approval and acceptance. . . . We're too afraid to put anything out in the world that could be imperfect. . . . [It is] deep fear of failing, making mistakes, and disappointing others."[7]

We see pressure to be perfect and fear of making mistakes demonstrated on *The Great British Baking Show.* Contestants square off to see who will become the "star baker." This amateur baking contest consists of technical and showstopper challenges that require contestants to make biscuits, cakes, cookies, and breads. The judges often introduce a technical challenge by saying, "The texture must be perfect, the flavors must harmonize beautifully, and each item must look exactly alike. We expect nothing less than perfection!" The stress on the contestants' faces is captivating. Relief finally comes when "Time's up!" is called, with some contestants collapsing on the floor as if steam from an Instant Pot pressure cooker had been released. Tears of disappointment flow when something is overbaked, flavors don't harmonize, or texture is doughy. We are glued to the screen, mouths watering to taste just one of those butter pecan tea biscuits laced with maple frosting. We are stunned that something so delicious looking is deemed a failure. Does it really have to be perfect to be a success? This baking show is just a form of entertainment, but what about real life? Do we needlessly pour on pressure with a similar standard of perfection?

Perfectionism feeds on self-doubt and frequently arises while viewing social media. We think, "Kalie has the perfect life traveling to other countries, so I need to travel to have the perfect life." Or "Milly is perfectly dressed in fashionable clothes, so I need to be fashionable too." Or "I'm just a brownie baker, a soup maker, and a perfect mom faker!" We may say, "Oh, I'm not a perfectionist," but call out to our family, "Everyone, come quick and clean the house! The bishop is coming, and we don't want to look like we live in a mess!" Are we focused on what others think of us, wanting to appear perfect to them? Elder Jeffrey R. Holland taught, "My brothers and sisters, except for Jesus, there have been no flawless performances on this earthly journey we are pursuing, so while in mortality let's strive for steady improvement without obsessing over what behavioral scientists call 'toxic perfectionism.' . . .

Every one of us aspires to a more Christlike life than we often succeed in living. If we admit that honestly and are trying to improve, we are not hypocrites; we are human."[8]

When we give in to perfectionism, we try to do the "perfecting" work that is not our role or even within our power. It is God's work. As someone once said to me, "I've learned to let God be God, to let Him do His work with me." It is God's work and glory "to bring to pass the immortality and eternal life of man" (Moses 1:39). It is Christ's work to enable us to be "at-one" with Him and our Father. Our Savior makes our journey back to Them achievable.

It is comforting that "God sent not his Son into the world to condemn the world; but that the world through him might be saved" (John 3:17). The Savior came to save us from our weaknesses, not to make us feel worse about them. Yet it is common to think and act as if God is condemning us, as if He is disappointed that we are not already perfect. However, God did not intend for us to have perfect abilities in this life but to embrace our *perfectibility*: the ability to eventually become perfect as He is.

President Russell M. Nelson helps us understand the verse "Be ye therefore perfect, even as your Father which is in heaven is perfect" (Matthew 5:48). He explains that the word *perfect* comes from the Greek word *teleios*, "which means 'complete.' *Teleios* is an adjective derived from the noun *telos*. . . . The infinitive form of the verb is *teleiono*, which means 'to reach a distant end, to be fully developed, . . . or to finish.'"[9] No one is complete and fully developed yet; we are only in the early stages of our eternal pilgrimage.

"It is a serious thing to live in a society of possible gods and goddesses. . . . There are no ordinary people," said C. S. Lewis.[10] God has granted us the ability to become like Him. That is our long-term goal, but what about our short-term goal of dealing with our current state of imperfection? We all feel the gap between where we are and where we need to go, much like pilgrims on the first days of their journey on the Camino de Santiago, wondering if they will ever reach their destination miles away. We learn from Elder Maxwell, "There is no way the Church can honestly describe where we must yet go and what we must yet do without creating a sense of immense distance. . . . The scriptural advice, 'Do not run faster or labor more than you have strength' (Doctrine and Covenants 10:4) suggests paced progress, much as God used seven creative periods in preparing man and this earth. There is a difference, therefore, between being 'anxiously engaged' and being over-anxious and thus underengaged."[11]

We need to remember that complacency is just as disruptive to God's plan as perfectionism. Can we be anxiously engaged in progression and at the same time be careful not to be overanxious about our quest for perfection? We must take one day at a time, throughout this life and beyond. How can we increase our focus on patience?

Focus on Patience: Progress instead of Perfection

In a TED Talk, Stanford University psychologist and author Carol Dweck spoke of a high school in Chicago where the students were required to complete eighty-four units to graduate. If students did not pass a unit, they did not receive a failing grade. Rather, their report card read "Not Yet." "Not Yet" implied that the students were still learning and still working to complete all that was required. Dweck said, "If you get a failing grade, you think, I'm nothing, I'm nowhere. But if you get the grade 'Not Yet,' you understand that you're on a learning curve. It gives you a path into the future."[12] The students and their teachers discovered that "Not Yet" grades helped students maintain motivation to keep working instead of giving up. They did not feel like failures but instead were at ease that there was still work to be done. A "Not Yet" mindset helped students accept tasks that were difficult; it created kids who were hardy, resilient, and persistent.

We can change our fixed mindset to what Dweck calls a *growth* mindset: one that is open to new growth and progress. Can we let it be OK that we are not finished and that there is still work to be done?

We are all in the state of "not yet"—we're not perfect *yet*, but we will be eventually. Right now we can focus on the progress we've made thus far and on our next steps forward. We can change our focus to who we are already (because of God's help) and be grateful instead of focusing on who we are not . . . yet. I accept that I have a "Not Yet" grade in every area of my life. There's a lot of work to be done. The tasks are endless, and I have miles to travel before I can sleep. But Christ gives me hope. His loving patience motivates me to keep trying. It motivates me to be patient with myself and others. And it motivates me to pour out my heart in gratitude for His loving companionship as we walk together.

Being patient helps us cherish others regardless of their imperfections. With patience, we let go of expectations that others have to be *better* in order for us to enjoy their company. With patience, we love more, we forgive more, we serve more, and we see the goodness in each other more. We simply find more joy in our relationships when our daily mortal walk is filled with patience.

I found joy one day when my daughter made me breakfast in bed for Mother's Day: burnt toast, cooked-to-death eggs, juice spilling out of the cup—the works! She presented me with a handwritten note that said, "I love you, Mom," and my heart melted. Another day she wrote a letter to me that said, "You are my best friend forever—my BFFFFFFFFFFFFFF," several extra *F*s emphasizing the "forever" part. So I didn't have the heart to get mad at her for making a mess in the kitchen. I was just happy to be her mom. Focusing on who our children *are* instead of who they *are not* enables us to treasure who they are today. It is a beautiful gift we give to one another—to feel cherished.

Someone once told me, "It's amazing how good others look when you look for the good. And it's amazing how bad others look when you look for the bad." So, what are we looking for? Let us look for the good today. Let us see the stepping stones of progress made this day.

We can be patient by taking one day at a time, trusting God's promises of our perfectibility, and looking for patient progress instead of immediate perfection.

Joy in the Process

Like the Creation process, we don't have to reach the final stage of our perfection before we experience God's love and feel God rejoice in who we have become thus far. We trust that the Lord would say to us what Alma said to his son Shiblon: "I say unto you, my son [or daughter], that I have had great joy in thee already, because of thy faithfulness and thy diligence, and thy patience" (Alma 38:3). Alma didn't find joy in his son at that moment for who he would become but for who he was already. Likewise, God finds joy in us now. I know God loves us too, no matter what our weaknesses and imperfections may be. Do we have a long way to go until we become like Him? Absolutely. He knows that, and so do we! But we can find joy by cherishing this day and knowing that God rejoices in our progress this day as well.

As parents we find joy in our children when they are small, still learning to walk and talk. We are not disappointed that they can't quote Shakespeare by their first birthday. We have no expectation that they will walk on their first attempt. None of us would dream of getting mad at or being disappointed with a one-year-old for falling down. Nor would we expect an infant to run around the block. We know better. Instead, we gather around them and cheer them on: "You can do it! Keep trying! You're almost there!" It is a joint effort. It is a partnership in growth and development. And we find joy in their every effort to become.

We also believe in a God who cheers us on. He not only loves us but finds joy in us with each day's diligent efforts. We can enjoy who we are today, knowing that the best is yet to come. Elder Dieter F. Uchtdorf said, "The lessons we learn from patience will cultivate our character, lift our lives, and heighten our happiness."[13]

Walking with Patience

A typical day on the Camino de Santiago began early in the morning. We packed our suitcases to be dropped off to a carrier service and packed a day pack with snacks, water, extra socks, and rain ponchos. We ate breakfast, stretched our legs and feet, grabbed our walking poles, and headed for the trail. The twelve to fifteen miles we walked each day took about five or six hours, which meant that we would arrive in the next town in the afternoon. I loved walking through all the villages, taking in the beautiful scenery, and meeting new people, but some days my feet got tired. Very tired. The arches in my feet would feel like fire. My husband would wait for me. He waited while I took extra stops at the snack shops to rest my feet. He waited while he rubbed my feet. He waited while I took an extra-long lunch. He waited while we sat on rocks along the trail. His patient words kept the journey enjoyable: "No problem, we will take as long as you need. There's no hurry. We can sit down and enjoy the scenery and meet more pilgrims." On those days we spent another four or five hours getting to our destination. But it was fun. Thanks to my husband's patience, we could enjoy our day's walk. There was no irritation for not arriving sooner. In fact, we met more people and learned more about their personal quests to draw closer to God. Being patient on our journey made it better, not worse.

Patience requires "waiting" on one another. Elder Robert D. Hales taught, "Waiting upon the Lord gives us a priceless opportunity to discover that there are many who wait upon us. Our children wait upon us to show patience, love, and understanding toward them. Our parents wait upon us to show gratitude and compassion. Our brothers and sisters wait upon us to be tolerant, merciful, and forgiving. Our spouses wait upon us to love them as the Savior has loved each one of us."[14] Can we let it be OK that we need to wait on one another? Waiting on one another makes our lives better, not worse. And it takes a lot of "waiting" to become our best selves.

My husband gave me a gift that summer we got married, when he was loving Spain . . . and me: an invitation to enjoy the creation of our marriage relationship. On the inside of our wedding rings, we had the Latin phrase *Incipit vita nova* engraved, meaning "A new life begins." We began a new life together, one of building a relationship—one day at a time. I love him for being patient and "waiting" with me. He often quotes Robert Browning:

> Grow old along with me!
> The best is yet to be,
> The last of life, for which the first was made:
> Our times are in His hand
> Who saith "A whole I planned,
> Youth shows but half; trust God: see all, nor be afraid!"[15]

Being patient has helped us enjoy the marriage we have, a relationship we cherish as it is today. Now, after thirty years of marriage, we look at each other and wonder if we have reached "day two" yet (like the seven-day Creation process of the earth).

We honor Christ as we walk with Him by focusing on His patience and accepting His invitation to be patient too. He doesn't expect us to run at top speed. He just asks us to keep on the path with Him, walking a steady, consistent pace forward. Elder Joseph B. Wirthlin reminds us, "Oh, it is wonderful to know that our Heavenly Father loves us—even with all our flaws! His love is such that even should we give up on ourselves, He never will. We see ourselves in terms of yesterday and today. Our Heavenly Father sees us in terms of forever. Although we might settle for less, Heavenly Father won't, for He sees us as the glorious beings we are capable of becoming."[16]

The next time we have feelings of self-doubt and consider giving up on ourselves, or the next time we consider giving up on someone we love, please remember that God will never give up on us. And He will never give up on the people we love.

Loving patience is powerful in cultivating relationships and personal growth and in overcoming self-doubt. It helps us find joy in the present moment. Patience helps us recognize how God has helped us

While my husband and I walked the Camino path, having patience made our journey enjoyable. Courtesy of author.

progress, and it gives us hope that He will continue to do so. We are reminded in Doctrine and Covenants 67:13, "Ye are not able to abide the presence of God now, . . . wherefore, continue in patience until ye are perfected."

On our personal journeys, we can imagine the Savior's invitation "Come, join me! Come warm your hands by the fire of my patience! See how I have blessed you already! Walk with me, and the glory of your potential will be made known to you—one day at a time."

Invitation: Focus on being patient with yourself and others in the process of becoming perfected. Let go of expectations that we or those we associate with have to be perfect in order to enjoy each other's company.

Think-in-ink journal challenge: Write down five ways God already has helped you become who you are at this point in your life.

Notes

1. Richard L. Evans, in Conference Report, October 1952, 95; quoted in Joseph B. Wirthlin, "Patience, a Key to Happiness," *Ensign*, May 1987, 33.
2. My husband also presents this idea in John R. Rosenberg, "The Syntax of Creation," *Humanities at BYU*, Fall 2013, 3.
3. For past talks given on the Creation process and personal progression, see Gaylamarie Rosenberg, "Allowing the Savior to Help Us with Our Imperfections" (address, Brigham Young University Women's Conference, Provo, UT, May 1, 2015), time codes 11:00–17:33, https://www.byutv.org/player/a35278a9-74cb-438e-9da9-0064dd820fa6/byu-womens-conference-gaylamarie-rosenberg-2015; and Rosenberg, "Gather to Be Perfected but Not Perfect" (address, Brigham Young University Women's Conference, Provo, UT, May 1, 2020), time codes 9:50–15:17, https://www.youtube.com/watch?v=11OkJjRF34k&t=26s.
4. Marvin J. Ashton, "Patience Is a Great Power" (Brigham Young University devotional, February 13, 1973), 5, speeches.byu.edu.
5. Neal A. Maxwell, "Patience" (Brigham Young University devotional, November 27, 1979), 1, 3, speeches.byu.edu.
6. Gerrit W. Gong, "Our Campfire of Faith," *Ensign*, November 2018, 42.
7. Brené Brown, *The Gifts of Imperfection: Let Go of Who You Think You're Supposed to Be and Embrace Who You Are* (Center City, MN: Hazelden, 2010), 56–57; italics in original.
8. Jeffrey R. Holland, "Be Ye Therefore Perfect—Eventually," *Ensign*, November 2017, 42.
9. Russell M. Nelson, "Perfection Pending," *Ensign*, November 1995, 86.
10. C. S. Lewis, *The Weight of Glory* (New York: HarperOne, 2001), 45–46.
11. Neal A. Maxwell, "Notwithstanding My Weakness," *Ensign*, November 1976, 12–13.
12. Carol Dweck, "The Power of Believing That You Can Improve," Ted Talk, November 2014, 10:11, https://www.ted.com/talks/carol_dweck_the_power_of_believing_that_you_can_improve.
13. Dieter F. Uchtdorf, "Continue in Patience," *Ensign*, May 2010, 59. For simplicity, the title "Elder" will be used throughout this work to refer to Dieter F.

Uchtdorf regardless of his position at the time he made each statement quoted herein.

14. Robert D. Hales, "Waiting upon the Lord: Thy Will Be Done," *Ensign*, November 2011, 73.
15. Robert Browning, "Rabbi Ben Ezra," in *Dramatis Personae* (London: Chapman and Hall, 1864), p. 77.
16. Joseph B. Wirthlin, "The Great Commandment," *Ensign*, November 2007, 29–30.

chapter two

FOCUS ON HIS CHARITY

Feelings of self-doubt come when we are critical of and negative about ourselves. The Savior can help as we focus on His charity, which helps us feel encouraged in times of discouragement. We can focus on how He sees us instead of on how we see ourselves.

I loved watching my toddlers staring and laughing at themselves in front of a big mirror. When they smiled, the mirror smiled back. When they frowned, it frowned back. When they danced, it danced with them. They were amazed by what they saw in front of them.

One of our greatest desires as parents is that our children have a positive image of themselves. Our heavenly parents want the same for us. I remember this statement attached to a picture of the Savior that a youth leader gave to me years ago: "The greatest gift I could give to you is for you to see yourself the way that I see you."

What do we see? Too often we look in the mirror and focus on flaws and imperfections. We may see someone who is weak, fearful, or untalented, someone with too many wrinkles and too much weight to lose. "My hair looks terrible!" "Am I always going to have puffy eyes?" "I'm not very smart." "The *only* talent I have is beating up on myself." "I have no discipline; I just can't stop eating all those yummy doughnuts." Or worse, "I'm not lovable. I'm a terrible person, so God has no interest in me."

The more we focus on weaknesses, the more weaknesses we see. We wouldn't dare criticize our friends to make them feel better. Nor would we motivate our children with a list of twenty things that we don't like about them. Yet we do it to ourselves too often.

Elder Dieter F. Uchtdorf said, "Some people can't get along with themselves. They criticize and belittle themselves all day long. . . . May I suggest that you reduce the rush and take a little extra time to get to know yourself better. . . . Learn to see yourself as Heavenly Father sees you—as His precious daughter or son with divine potential."[1]

How can we see ourselves as God sees us?

Seeing Ourselves as Christ Sees Us

The Apostle Paul suggests an answer in 1 Corinthians 13. Following the verses on the characteristics of charity, in verse 12 we read, "For now we see through a glass, darkly; but then face to face: now I know in part; but then shall I know even as also I am known." Paul did not use the word *glass* as we have it in the King James Version of the Bible. He used the Greek word for *mirror*. Today we have mirrors that give us a crystal-clear image of ourselves. But in Paul's day, polished metal functioned as a mirror, offering only a blurry reflection of the viewer.[2]

Another way of reading this verse is "Right now, you see yourself unclearly—like seeing a blurry reflection of yourself on polished brass. You see only part of your true self now, but when you see Christ face to face, then shall you know yourself even as you are known by Him."

Paul explains this verse in the context of charity, the "pure love of Christ" (Moroni 7:47), the greatest of all spiritual gifts. He gives us a key to understanding how to know ourselves as we are known by God: if we can recognize God's charity for us and share charity with others, we will begin to understand how God sees us. When we understand Christ's pure love for us, we look at ourselves differently. When we share His charity with others, we achieve a refined character like His. Then we look in the mirror and see a clear reflection of Christ in our countenance (see Alma 5:19). Charity is the mirror through which we see ourselves clearly.

In medieval and Renaissance art, a mirror could represent either truth or pride. "Mirror, mirror on the wall, who's the fairest of them all?" asks the vain queen in *Snow White*. Here, the mirror symbolizes the vice of pride. But mirrors are also used as a symbol to see truth about oneself.

Because they were polished brass, ancient mirrors gave people only a fuzzy image of themselves. Courtesy of Wellcome Trust. https://wellcomecollection.org/works/kkhnay4w.

Seeing ourselves through Christ's loving eyes enables us to see the truth about our divine nature. As we accept His truth, we see ourselves with more positive and compassionate feelings. God wants us to know the truth about who we really are. "Remember the worth of souls is great in the sight of God" (Doctrine and Covenants 18:10). Your worth is great, even if you don't see it. Jesus Christ saves us not only from imperfection but also from our imperfect understanding of ourselves. We begin to understand our worth and potential when we understand His pure love (or His charity) for us.

How do we experience Christ's charity? How does sharing His charity help us see ourselves more clearly? First, we need to ask ourselves what blinds us to God's love and the truth of our divine nature.

Discouragement versus Encouragement

God's abundant charity contrasts with the adversary's unwillingness to love. The Savior encourages; Satan discourages. The Savior nurtures faith; Satan cultivates fear. The Savior promises to connect us to God; Satan aims to disconnect us from Him (and all edifying relationships). Sheri Dew reminds us, "Satan wants us to see ourselves as the world sees us, not as the Lord sees us, because the world's mirror . . . distorts and minimizes us. Satan tells us we're not good enough. Not smart enough. Not thin enough. Not cute enough. Not clever enough. Not *anything* enough. And that is a big, fat, devilish lie."[3] Satan wants us to doubt ourselves. He tries to blur the image we see of our divine nature. How does he do it? Some of Satan's cunning ways were described by Denise Lindberg at the 2015 BYU Women's Conference:

> Once upon a time, Satan announced that he was thinking of retiring from business and would offer all his diabolical inventions for sale to anyone who would pay the price.
>
> On the day of the sale, the tools were all attractively displayed, despite the ugliness of most of them. Malice, hatred, jealousy,

> sensuality, deceit, and all the other instrumentalities of evil—each was marked with its price. Apart from the rest lay a plain wedge-shaped tool, much worn and priced higher than any of the others. Someone asked Satan what it was.
>
> "That's Discouragement," was the reply.
>
> "Why have you priced such a simple tool so high?"
>
> "Because," Satan replied, "it is more useful to me than any of the others. I can pry open and get inside a man's consciousness with that when I could not get near him with any of the others. . . . It is much worn because I have used it on nearly everybody, yet few, very few, know that it belongs to me."
>
> And it came to pass that Satan's price for Discouragement was so high that it was never sold. He still owns it and is still using it.[4]

With the wedge in hand, Satan remains fully employed. The adversary wants us to be distraught, distracted, and discouraged. We all experience discouragement. We all wish we were better. No one enjoys falling short. The problem is not being disappointed or discouraged but *staying* discouraged. There is hope. And we have help!

Can we catch ourselves when we are being critical of and negative about ourselves? Honest awareness of our weaknesses is one thing. Relentless self-negativity is something else. When we constantly criticize ourselves, we are hurting ourselves, not helping ourselves.

When we are negative about and critical of ourselves, we make ourselves vulnerable to discouragement. For example, Jordan tells himself he is too dumb to go to school, so he drops out instead of accepting his teacher's offer to help. Every time Janice looks in the mirror, she tells herself she is not pretty enough to get married, so she stops going to social activities. Jeff thinks he is a terrible person for viewing pornography, so he avoids seeking help. Jen thinks she is not a good mother when her child makes one bad choice after another, so she gives up on herself and on him.

Self-doubt increases when we are pessimistic about our possibilities. Negative self-talk dampens our courage to act. We focus on what isn't instead of what can be. Negativity blinds us to the confidence, hope, joy, and peace found in God's love. Brent L. Top and Wendy C. Top shared, "If we allowed ourselves to feel as much of Christ's love as we would want others to feel, we could set ourselves free from the chains of self-contempt that enslave us and smother our happiness and potential."[5] We want others to feel loved and encouraged by Christ so that they can overcome self-doubt. What if we allow ourselves that same gift of love?

When we are negative and critical with ourselves, we lose sight of our divine worth and God's love for us. My niece shared her battle with perfectionism:

> I had a belief that I had to be perfect or no one would love me or want to be around me. I'm now learning that this belief is false. Yes, we are supposed to be perfect *eventually*, but all that is asked of us right now is to do our best *now*. Perfectionism is a long-term, unreachable-here-on-earth goal. I just have to keep reminding myself that I am lovable with my faults and mistakes. I don't have to be perfect to deserve love. I am lovable simply because I am a Daughter of God. We all make mistakes. That's what makes the Atonement of Jesus Christ such an amazing gift. We can repent and do better. I'm so thankful for such a selfless gift from my Savior.[6]

Our weaknesses do not make us less lovable in God's eyes. We don't have to be perfect to deserve love. We *are* lovable! The good news from our Savior is that He loves us! He loves us even when we make mistakes. He loves us even when we sin, even if we keep repeating the same sin. (Because of His love, He wants us to become our best selves—which requires repentance.) He loves us when we feel unattractive, unintelligent, untalented, incapable, and inadequate. The Redeemer of the world still loves us when we don't feel good about ourselves. He is with us. Always.

A young adult said to me, "If God loves us just the way we are, then I don't have to worry about getting any better, because I can worry about perfection after I die." I don't think she got the right message. "Be perfect even as I" (3 Nephi 12:48) does not mean "eat, drink, and be merry, for tomorrow [ye] die" (2 Nephi 28:7)—and then be perfect. Personal growth and refinement *are* essential during our mortal pilgrimage.

We are made in God's image with potential to become like Him—which means we have a lot of work to do! God knows that. And so do we. Is God's love for us less because we are not perfect like Him? No. Nothing could be further from the truth! In 1 John 4:9, 16–17, we learn, "In this was manifested the love of God toward us, because . . . God sent his only begotten Son into the world, that we might *live through him*. . . . And we have known and believed the love that God hath to us. God is love; and he that dwelleth in love dwelleth in God, and God in him. Herein is our love made perfect" (italics added). God sent us to earth to experience growth from a state of weakness. That is why He sent His Son—to witness of Their love for us.

When we have doubt about who we are and what we can become, we can remember that the most powerful antidote for discouragement is God's encouragement. The Latin root of the word *courage* is *cor*—that is, "heart." When we have courage, we have the heart to act. To encourage is to hearten—to inspire with courage. To discourage is to dishearten—to deprive of courage or confidence. Satan seeks to destroy our confidence with discouragement. But Christ's encouragement is more powerful. His love gives us courage to act, to handle adversity, and to stretch our capability, and it grants us the motivation to become our best selves.

My sister Karen taught me the power of Christ's encouragement. Karen saw herself through the reflection of Christ's pure love. She knew that she belonged to Him and that He would take care of her. She endured cancer, congestive heart failure, spinal surgery, a neuromuscular disease, a heart transplant, and kidney failure. For twenty years she fought serious health challenges, and every time I asked her what gave her the strength and peace to keep going, she replied, "Christ helps me deal with pain. He gives me comfort and peace that everything is going to be OK. He fills in the gaps where I need help, and He helps me to be happy now."

Karen's enthusiasm and happiness were contagious. She inspired everyone to look for the positives in life and acknowledge the depths of God's love and strength. She often said, "It takes more energy to be negative than to be positive. I don't have the energy to be discouraged. It doesn't do me any good, and I enjoy life more being positive."

No one would have judged Karen if she complained about her challenges. She had reason to be discouraged. She could have said, "I can't do anything. There's nothing good about my life. My body is the worst. I'm hopeless." But she didn't. She chose to focus on the positive. I heard her say, "I can do all the things that matter most to me right here from my bed: I can nurture my husband. I can love and support my children. I can do family history work and family scrapbooks." And she was happy. God's love is powerful. It is encouraging. His love helps us to be optimistic about who we are, what we can do, and what we have.

Karen experienced Christ's charity in a variety of ways. The Lord strengthened her to "bear up [her] burdens with ease" and to "submit cheerfully and with patience" (Mosiah 24:15). Christ took upon Him her pains and sicknesses, His bowels filled with mercy, to succor her according to her infirmities (see Alma 7:11–12). Karen found power and peace in Christ's charity. She reminded us not to let discouragement block our view of God's encouragement.

We choose where to focus our attention when we get discouraged. Again, we all get discouraged from time to time. Recognizing Christ's love helps us not to *stay* discouraged.

Recognizing Christ's Charity

Do we recognize the many ways we experience God's love? The possibilities are endless. We can explain that the "pure love" of Christ is charity. But how do we experience Christ's charity?

In his book *Eclipse of God*, philosopher Martin Buber explains that faith in the reality of God is not fostered by explaining God with reason, logic, or science, but it is enhanced by experiencing God through a relationship with Him. To experience God is to feel the presence of His love and His strength. Faith must speak of love.[7] In other words, faith is not fostered by just proving that God is real but by *experiencing* His love and strength.

A moment when I understood more clearly God's love for me happened while taking my husband to the airport. He had a few minutes before his departure, and I took the opportunity to pick his brain for ideas about a talk I was preparing. He looked at me and said, "Gaylamarie, I think grace is best understood as Christ's charity for us." We discussed more ideas, and then he was off to Spain. On the drive home, I kept thinking about charity. I had never considered that Heavenly Father and Jesus Christ manifest charity in a variety of ways to us all the time. I had always thought of their love but not about ways they exemplify charity, such as through grace. But thinking of the many attributes of charity described by Paul in 1 Corinthians 13 ("charity suffereth long," "is kind," "thinketh no evil," and "beareth," "believeth," "hopeth," and "endureth all things") enhanced my understanding of what Christ's charity frequently offers me. At that moment, my heart was filled with gratitude as I thought about how Christ showed kindness to me, was patient with me, suffered for me, believed in me, bore my pain, endured my shortcomings, and had great hope for me. It was an unforgettable moment that reminded me of how I experience God's love again and again in my life.

Moroni spoke of Christ's charity when he prayed to the Lord in our behalf: "And now I know that this love which thou hast had for the children of men is charity" (Ether 12:34). President Jean B. Bingham said, "Jesus Christ is the perfect embodiment of charity. His premortal offering to be our Savior, . . . His supernal gift of the Atonement, and His continual efforts to bring us back to our Heavenly Father are the ultimate expressions of charity."[8]

When discouragement hits, we can stop and recognize how we experience Christ's charity. Paul urges, "[May] the Lord direct your hearts into the love of God, and into the patient waiting for Christ" (2 Thessalonians 3:5).

How do you experience God's love and strength? Each person experiences God's charity differently, often manifested through the Holy Spirit. You may relate to these possibilities of how I have experienced God's love:

- Feeling loved and at peace when my family members have passed away. (When my father, mother, sister, and brother died, I felt an undeniable abundance of love and peace during those difficult times.)
- Receiving impressions that God loves me while praying in the temple. (For me, whisperings from heaven of "I love you" come most clearly in sacred spaces.)
- Being uplifted while listening to beautiful music. ("In This Very Room," composed by Ron Harris and Carol Harris, and "O Divine Redeemer," composed by Charles Gounod, are a couple of songs that uplift me every time.)
- Feeling loved while reading the voice of the Lord in the scriptures. (One of my favorite scriptures is 3 Nephi 17:17: "No one can conceive of the joy which filled our souls at the time we heard [Jesus] pray for *us* unto the Father.")
- Receiving a witness of God's love through the words of living prophets. (Elder Uchtdorf's words "Always remember—you matter to Him" were a powerful reminder of how God felt about me.)[9]
- Feeling God's forgiveness as I have repented and known I am loved and accepted. (One of the many times I have felt this is when I am impatient with my family. After repenting, I feel motivated to be more patient!)

- Being strengthened and motivated to keep trying as I humbly pray. (I get discouraged if I teach a weak lesson to my college students, but prayer gives me the peace and motivation to try again.) Prayer is powerful! When was the last time you asked God how He feels about you? When was the last time you pleaded to Him, "Please help me. Please help me understand your love and your will for me"? You may have to wait. But He will answer.
- Receiving encouragement through another person letting me know God was aware of me. (A phone call from a friend at just the right moment was a tender mercy.)
- Writing in my journal to clarify my thoughts. (As a missionary, I wrote down five ways I had felt God's hand in my life each day. This motivated me to carefully review the day's events. The more I wrote, the more my ability to recognize God's love for me increased. This helped me as a missionary and continues to help me now.)

What can we do to increase our awareness of God's pure love? When discouragement hits, we can focus our hearts and minds on Christ's encouragement through scripture study (including words from living prophets), prayer, temple attendance, and journal writing. These suggestions perhaps sound too simple and familiar, like when Elisha told Naaman to go wash in the Jordan River seven times (see 2 Kings 5:10–14). Sometimes what we need is not "some great thing" (verse 13) but simple daily spiritual habits that remind us that God loves us.

Our daily devotions allow us to store up surplus strength for the "lean years" of possible stress and disappointment. We can build a deep reservoir of faith, hope, and confidence in God's love.

I was inspired by something author Fiona Givens said to me: "Each member of the Godhead works collaboratively—in perfect unity and harmony to minister to our needs." I love the thought that we are surrounded by love from each member of the Godhead. We should feel important—to think that they are mindful of us, that they jointly *plan* for and counsel together about us, that they minister to us in a variety of ways to help us accomplish our mission here on earth.

I also relate to the strength Enos acquired from his father: "He taught me . . . in the nurture and admonition of the Lord . . . ; and the words which I had often heard my father speak concerning eternal life . . . sunk deep into my heart" (Enos 1:1, 3). My father's faith created a deep reservoir of strength for me as well. Every week in home evening, he said, "I know Heavenly Father loves you. I know the Savior loves you. And we love you too!" Week after week, year after year, I was reminded of God's love for me; I heard it so often that I believed it—and still do! It was easy for me to trust in the love of my heavenly parents because I felt love from my earthly parents. We give a beautiful gift to one another when we love, because we get a glimpse of what it's like to be loved by the Lord. (If you didn't grow up with a father who reminded you often of God's love, you can ask God directly. He will tell you. He is *your* Father!)

When you feel discouraged, Christ's charity can help you feel encouraged. The more we increase our focus on how Christ sees us instead of on how we see ourselves, the more we will recognize His love for us. His love motivates us to stop being critical of ourselves and to be more loving, understanding, and compassionate with ourselves and others. Experiencing Christ's encouragement also motivates us to share His love and strength with others.

Sharing Christ's Charity

How does sharing Christ's charity help us see ourselves and others through a less critical eye?

First, sharing the love of the Lord helps us overcome self-doubt as we think less about our weaknesses and more about how we can love and bless others.

I heard someone say, "When you don't feel good about yourself, others suffer." Why? Others miss out on our loving-kindness when we are mired in self-doubt. We miss precious opportunities to love and be loved because doubt restrains us from interacting. We avoid conversation because negative self-talk convinces us we are not worthy of someone's time, or because we fear they have negative thoughts about us too. Our fear makes us too shy to share ourselves. When we encounter negative self-talk, we must change our focus. While serving as Young Women General President, Susan W. Tanner shared an experience when her mother taught her to change her focus:

> I remember well the insecurities I felt as a teenager with a bad case of acne. I tried to care for my skin properly. My parents helped me get medical attention. For years I even went without eating chocolate and all the greasy fast foods around which teens often socialize, but with no obvious healing consequences. It was difficult for me at that time to fully appreciate this body which was giving me so much grief. But my good mother taught me a higher law. Over and over she said to me, "You must do everything you can to make your appearance pleasing, but the minute you walk out the door, *forget yourself and start concentrating on others.*"
>
> There it was. She was teaching me the Christlike principle of selflessness. . . . When we become other-oriented, or selfless, we develop an inner beauty of spirit that glows in our outward appearance. This is how we make ourselves in the Lord's image rather than the world's and receive His image in our countenances.[10]

I love how her mother told her to take care of herself—to work on being the best person she could be—and then to leave the weight of worrying about her perceived inadequacies at the door. She could forget about herself and turn her focus to others.

Sharing charity becomes the mirror that helps us see our connection with God, others, and ourselves. With selfless actions and selfless attitudes, we become more godlike. Those selfless moments become moments when we see ourselves more clearly—in a more Christlike manner—and receive His image in our countenances. Loving others refines our character.

Second, seeing others through the eyes of God helps us feel warmth and compassion for one another and for ourselves. We learn to see beyond imperfections as we love others and love ourselves—for God.

One mother shared her feelings when she became frustrated with her son's difficult behavior:

> When our son was in junior high school, there were moments when his behavior was difficult to manage. I loved him but didn't *like* him—at least not his behavior. And I let God know how I felt about it! I didn't feel successful as a mother and felt bad about my feelings toward my son. I remember pouring out my heart to the Lord for help, and the clear and strong impression I received was "You may not feel like you can love him for you right now, but can you *love him for me*? Can you put away your irritations and frustrations and just love him for me right now? Are you willing to do that?"
>
> I remember thinking, "Of course I'm willing to do that for You—to forget about myself and do it for You." I *was* willing to love my son for God. That was a turning point in how I felt about him, how I felt about his life, and how I interacted with him. Something beautiful happened with how I saw my son's goodness. I saw him and myself differently. And I could feel greater love from God for both of us. I'm thankful for the loving relationship I share with my son today.

Can we start by asking ourselves if we are willing to love another for *Him*—for our Father in Heaven? Can we do it for Him? Can we love that person for Heavenly Father even if we can't for us—even if we are still in the process of letting go of any hurt, pain, and frustration?

Can we love for Christ?

"The place to start is with our own hearts," says President Henry B. Eyring. "What we want with all our hearts will determine in large degree whether we can claim our right to the companionship of the Holy Ghost, without which there can be no spiritual nourishing. We can begin today to try to see those we are to nourish as our Heavenly Father sees them and so feel some of what He feels for them."[11] Seeing others through the eyes of God allows us to feel compassion for one another, which also helps us identify how we experience warmth and compassion from God.

Experiencing Christ's charity often happens when we extend His love to others. In Moroni 7:48 we read, "Pray unto the Father with all the energy of heart, that ye may be filled with this love." If we sincerely desire to love for Him, those prayers will be answered. He will help us love for Him, and beautiful things will happen to our own hearts in the process.

One of my favorite movies, *Always*, portrays the life of a firefighter pilot who dies and comes back in spirit to watch over his girlfriend. He tries to teach her that "the only pain we take with us into the next life is the *love* we withhold in this life." I have often thought of that sentence and wonder if I am withholding love from others. After several deaths in my family, I realized that the time we have to love others on our mortal journey is very short. No time to waste! The time to love is now!

Third, sharing Christ's charity helps us prevent and heal from sins, mistakes, and suffering. In 1 Peter 4:8 we read, "And above all things have fervent charity among yourselves: for charity *shall cover* the multitude of sins" (italics added). The Joseph Smith Translation replaces the words "shall cover" with "preventeth." Charity prevents us from acting poorly, and charity "covers" or helps us heal from wrongdoing or mistakes. I like to think of charity as healing power. Charity heals all kinds of wounds, pain, sin, and suffering.

Focusing on Christ's charity can also heal us from a negative mindset. Pessimism can turn to optimism. Negativity about our vices can turn to gratitude about our virtues. Despair about our inadequacies can turn to hope about our possibilities. And discouraging words about our flaws and imperfections can turn to encouraging words about our attributes and blessings.

Christ can help us change the way we think. He can help us change our attitudes about ourselves. Christ's pure love can heal our hearts and heal our minds . . . on His time. When we feel weighed down, "may Christ lift [us] up, and may his . . . mercy and long-suffering, and the hope of his glory and of eternal life, rest in [our] *mind[s]* forever" (Moroni 9:25; italics added).

Nothing is more powerful and healing than pure love.

My mother taught me about charity and healing. Because of a massive stroke, she was left with unrecognizable speech and no movement on the right side of her body. For five years she spoke all the time, but not with sounds anyone could understand. On many occasions, when I went to the care center where she lived, I found her visiting with the other residents in their rooms. She believed that she was the welcoming committee for all new residents and took it upon herself to show love and concern for them. I watched her love others with her smile, her facial expressions, and her gestures of compassion. That doesn't sound unusual for a friendly and outgoing soul like my mother, but to extend herself to others without recognizable speech made her conversations extraordinary. She wanted others to feel loved and cared for—whether they could understand her or not.

Many painful and difficult days came after my mother's stroke, but my heart was touched as I saw God's love heal her mind. Instead of being in the depths of despair about her condition, she was happy. She could have been upset about losing her ability to walk and talk and being left with only three arthritic, crippled fingers to eat with. Instead, she decided to share the joy she felt with others. Watching her often brought tears to my eyes. Her positive mindset was evidence of God caring about our optimism. Christ's encouragement helps us find joy in the life we have and deal productively with discouragement.

My mother taught me a critical lesson: it doesn't matter what our disabilities, weaknesses, or imperfections may be—we can always find great joy by partaking of and sharing Christ's charity.

God's Mirror

Describing the symbolism of the mirror in the writings of medieval Christian thinkers, author Sabine Melchior-Bonnet wrote that "all creation has its origin in the mirror of God" and that "it is precisely because there is resemblance or likeness that there is the possibility of knowing oneself."[12] It is possible to know—to see—ourselves clearly in God's mirror because we are His children, made in His image and reflection. To imitate His divine character is to reflect the heavenly light of our own divine nature. Instead of seeing ourselves "through a glass, darkly" (1 Corinthians 13:12), our eyes are opened to who we are and what we may become when we view life through the lens of God's charity.

God's charity is powerful; it helps us find happiness in the life we have and helps us transform discouraging thoughts to encouraging ones. Recognizing Christ's charity brings clarity about our divine nature and motivates us to move forward in our personal refinement. Sharing charity helps us to think less about our weaknesses and more about loving for Christ. We become more selfless in our attitudes and actions. We learn to see beyond imperfections and love others—and ourselves—for God. In Doctrine and Covenants 88:125 we read, "And above all things, clothe yourselves with the bond of charity, as with a mantle, which is the bond of perfectness and peace." If we do this, then we shall see and know ourselves as we are seen and known by Him in whose image we are made.

Can we challenge negative and critical thoughts about ourselves by looking at ourselves through the lens of God's pure love? Being grounded in His love changes how we feel about ourselves: "That he would grant you, according to the riches of his glory, to be strengthened with might by his Spirit in the inner man; that Christ may dwell in your hearts by faith; that ye, being rooted and grounded in love, may be able to . . . know the love of Christ" (Ephesians 3:16–19).

On the last day of our Camino de Santiago experience, the students had a chance to share their feelings about their journey. The comment that I heard most frequently was that they felt the love of the Lord through the love of each other. One student said, "Angels that protect and guide us are often the people that we interact with every day. Each day I walked the Camino, I spoke with someone who said something I needed to hear that day." When we are in need of love and encouragement, our Savior sends help.

As we walk along our personal Caminos in life, the most powerful encouragement we receive is "I love you" from God above. When we are negative and critical toward ourselves, I imagine Christ calling out to us, saying, "Come join me by the fire. Warm your hands with my compassion. I love you. I see your goodness. I see your heart. I see the glorious being you are capable of becoming. Stop the criticism and see yourself as I see you. 'As the Father hath loved me, so have I loved you: continue ye in my love' [John 15:9]."

Invitation: Focus on how Christ sees you with His pure love. Focus on how you experience His love, strength, and encouragement.

Think-in-ink journal challenge: Write down ten ways you have experienced Christ's charity. Also write two things you'd like to do to increase your awareness of His love for you.

Notes

1. Dieter F. Uchtdorf, "Of Things That Matter Most," *Ensign*, November 2010, 22.
2. See Thomas A. Wayment, *The New Testament: A Translation for Latter-day Saints* (Provo, UT: Religious Studies Center, Brigham Young University; Salt Lake City: Deseret Book, 2019), 307.
3. Sheri Dew, "Knowing Who You Are—and Who You Have Always Been" (address, Brigham Young University Women's Conference, Provo, UT, May 4, 2001); italics in original.
4. Denise Posse Lindberg, "Perfection's Path: Do Your Best, Trust Christ with the Rest" (address, Brigham Young University Women's Conference, Provo, UT, May 1, 2015), https://www.byutv.org/player/0ba64591-e4df-4455-aad4-5835589a5e28/byu-womens-conference-denise-posse-lindberg-2015.
5. Brent L. Top and Wendy C. Top, *Finding Inner Peace: Lessons Learned from Trying Too Hard* (American Fork, UT: Covenant Communications, 2015), 71.
6. Laura H. Vogelsberg, email message to author, May 28, 2020.
7. See Martin Buber, *Eclipse of God: Studies in the Relation between Religion and Philosophy* (Princeton: Princeton University Press, 2016), xii–xv.
8. Jean B. Bingham, "I Will Bring the Light of the Gospel into My Home," *Ensign*, November 2016, 6.
9. Dieter F. Uchtdorf, "You Matter to Him," *Ensign*, November 2011, 22.
10. Susan W. Tanner, "The Sanctity of the Body," *Ensign*, November 2005, 15; italics added.
11. Henry B. Eyring, "Feeding His Lambs," *Ensign*, February 2008, 6.
12. Sabine Melchior-Bonnet, *The Mirror: A History*, trans. Katharine H. Jewett (New York: Routledge, 2002), 113, 112.

chapter three

FOCUS ON HIS POWER

Feelings of self-doubt come from the fear of not being enough. The Savior has the power to make our weak things strong. He will empower us with strength. As we trust in Him and focus more on what we can do instead of what we can't do, our confidence will wax strong in Him.

Three months into my mission in Guatemala, I was assigned to train a new missionary from the missionary training center (MTC), manage a proselyting area, and train the leaders in thirteen wards and branches in welfare principles. I was willing to accept any assignment from my mission president, but I had one major problem: I couldn't speak Spanish well. I had no idea what Guatemalans were saying to me, and they had no idea what I was trying to say to them!

I called my district and zone leaders and asked them to call our mission president to see if he had made a mistake. I told them, "Our president must be kidding! You know I can't speak Spanish. I've only been here for three months." I knew I did not have the ability to do what was asked of me.

And my leaders agreed with me. "Yeah, you're right," they said. "Your Spanish is *muy malo* ('really bad')!"

My district leader called our mission president, who asked him not to question his decision. My zone leader also called and got the same response. I was scared to death when I heard my mission president was serious, and I spent the day crying over my feelings of inadequacy.

On the day of transfers, I approached my mission president—a former colonel in the Marines—and said, "President, I would never doubt your inspiration, but are you sure you weren't thinking of someone else?"

He looked at me and sternly said, "Sister, I had the same concerns about your ability as you have, so I went back to the Lord, and He got mad at me for having doubts about you."

Then he turned and walked off. I was speechless. As he walked away, I thought, "Wow, the Lord really knows who I am! He thinks I can do this! If He wants me to do this, then He must be serious about helping me."

Then an inspired question came to my mind: "Are you willing?" Hearing from my mission president that the Lord had confidence in me helped me realize that it didn't matter if I thought I had the ability or not. What mattered was my willingness. Was I willing to give my best effort with whatever ability I had? Could I trust that He believed in me more than I believed in myself and that He would enhance my ability?

That experience challenged me to focus on what I *could* do instead of what I *couldn't* do. Hearing from my mission president that the Lord did not doubt *my* ability gave me determination to show God that I did not doubt *His* ability to help me.

In the weeks that followed, I prayed and worked hard to learn Spanish. The assurance that the Lord believed in me, knew me, and loved me helped me think less about my weaknesses and more about doing my best to serve Him. He helped me learn the language in order to do what He asked me to do. I still don't speak beautiful Spanish, but I know that as a missionary many years ago, I had divine assistance to complete an assignment that seemed impossible. Was my effort perfect? Absolutely not, but I was willing, and the Lord used my willingness to do His work.

Fear of Not Being Enough

We often find ourselves in situations in which we fear our abilities are not enough. Dan Baker, psychologist and author of *What Happy People Know*, explains that one of the greatest enemies of happiness is fear: "Contemporary fear, I've found, almost always fits into one of two categories: *fear of not having enough* and *fear of not being enough*. . . . But focusing on weaknesses, like focusing on anything else that's negative, just reinforces fear."[1] What we focus on matters. Focusing on our fears fuels self-doubt.

We may hear phrases like these from others—or have these thoughts ourselves: "I can't." "I'm not capable enough." "I don't know enough." "I can't do it—I'm not smart enough, talented enough, beautiful enough, good enough." We simply fear we are not *enough*. What does *enough* even mean? Sufficient? Sufficient for what? To do everything perfectly? Not likely. To do something of value? Absolutely!

Fear and self-doubt are accomplices in preventing us to act; they wreak havoc on our emotions and thoughts. Are you afraid of failure? Do you think you are the only one who feels that way? Think again. Everyone experiences some sort of defeat.

Fear can be induced by our own thoughts or by the comments of others. Here are a few famous people you'll recognize whose abilities were doubted by others:

- Thomas Edison was told he was "too stupid to learn anything."
- Albert Einstein didn't start speaking until he was four or reading until he was seven, and he was labeled by some as mentally handicapped.
- Abraham Lincoln failed in several business attempts and lost eight elections.
- Walt Disney was told that he "lacked imagination and had no great ideas."
- Theodor Geisel (Dr. Seuss) submitted his first book to twenty-seven publishers, all of whom rejected it, before it was published.
- Vincent van Gogh sold just one painting during his lifetime.
- Michael Jordan was cut from his high school basketball team.
- Steven Spielberg was rejected twice by a university cinematic arts program.
- Elvis Presley was told, "You ain't goin' nowhere, son. You ought to go back to drivin' a truck."[2]

All these people could have believed they were not enough, but they chose not to. And their success stories are amazing! They refused to let fear or doubt hold them back. We see common examples of the boy who sits on the bench game after game, year after year, but keeps practicing hard anyway; the teenager who is teased about her appearance but decides to be friendly anyway; the young adult who is rejected for a date for the tenth time but keeps building friendships anyway; the father who is laid off from employment for the third time but remains optimistic anyway; or the mother whose child was thrown in jail for the second time but refuses to feel like a failure, knowing she has done her best as a parent.

All of us have to choose not to give in to the fear of not being enough. President Thomas S. Monson shared the letter of a student who refused rejection from a college:

> *Dear Admissions Officer:*
>
> *I am in receipt of your rejection of my application. As much as I would like to accommodate you, I find I cannot accept it. I have already received four rejections from other colleges, and this number is, in fact, over my limit. Therefore, I must reject your rejection—and will appear for classes on September first.*

President Monson added, "I don't know the outcome of that student's letter, but there are many examples in life of those who rise from failure to success."[3]

We can choose how we will respond to our feelings of self-doubt. Most importantly, we can choose to change our focus from fear to faith in our God in Heaven, who will help us.

From Fear to Faith

BYU president Kevin J Worthen explained the difference between focusing on fear and focusing on faith:

> For far too many, this fear comes in the form of the false belief that you are not acceptable to God, that you are so flawed because of past mistakes or current inadequacies that you are beyond the reach of the refining and redeeming power of Jesus Christ. . . .
>
> . . . If we want to decrease . . . fear in our lives, we need to increase our faith in the Lord Jesus Christ. So when fear threatens

> to overwhelm us, we should focus less on those fears and more on increasing our faith in Him who admonishes us to "look unto [Him] in every thought; doubt not, fear not" [Doctrine and Covenants 6:36].[4]

Can we challenge false beliefs that we are not acceptable to God and believe in His love for us and desire to help us? When we focus on faith in the redeeming power of Jesus Christ, our fears slip back into the shadows. Moroni reminds us, "I would exhort you that ye deny not the power of God; for he worketh by power, according to the faith of the children of men" (Moroni 10:7). Christ works by power. He has the power to make our weak things strong: "I give unto men weakness that they may be humble; and my grace is sufficient for all men that humble themselves before me; for if they humble themselves before me, and have faith in me, then will I make weak things become strong unto them" (Ether 12:27). Christ will empower us!

When we feel that we are not enough or that we don't have the ability to tackle a task, can we remember that Christ has the power to strengthen our abilities? He desires that we take advantage of the precious opportunity to access His power because we are good enough to help! We are enough to love. We are enough to support, even when we whine and complain about our fears. We are enough for Him to give us attention, even though we are only one of His many children. Our abilities are enough for Him to work with, no matter how weak we may feel. We are enough for Him to grant us power to strengthen our capabilities. But the Lord requires a willing heart and a willing mind to do His will.

You may question, "If my weakness is impatience, do I have confidence that a perfectly patient God can lift me toward Him?" "If my prayers are lazy, do I believe that He, in whose name I pray, can enliven my daily devotions?" "If I am judgmental of others, what are the chances that the Perfect Judge, if asked, can help me replace my defective justice for more mercy?" Again, we are enough for God to help us; we just need to turn our hearts to Him and seek His will.

As we focus on the Savior's power to help us, our fears will diminish. Elder Dieter F. Uchtdorf taught:

> Rather than dwelling on the immensity of our challenges, would it not be better to focus on the infinite greatness, goodness, and absolute power of our God . . . ?
>
> . . . We need not be paralyzed by fear. . . . Instead, we can move forward with faith, courage, determination, and trust in God as we approach the challenges and opportunities ahead. . . .
>
> . . . Therefore, let us set aside our fears and live instead with joy, humility, hope, and a bold confidence that the Lord is with us.[5]

How can we obtain that bold confidence? Psychotherapist Dan Baker suggests a starting point:

> Courage, they say, is not the lack of fear, but the ability to take action in spite of it. But where does that ability come from? What power grants the strength to overcome the sick, shaky feeling of fear?
>
> Only one power is that strong: love.
>
> . . . Fear impels us to survive, and love enables us to thrive. . . .
>
> . . . Nobody's perfect, and if you're afraid you're not good enough to be loved, you'll always find an imperfection to feed that fear.
>
> Happy people don't fight the imperfection. They fight the fear. Nobody overcomes this fear easily. The fear of not being enough is strong. But it's not as strong as love.[6]

Love is stronger than fear. If we are still on day one of our development—like the first day of the seven-day Creation process—we are good enough to be loved by God. Second Timothy 1:7 teaches us, "For God hath not given us the spirit of fear; but of power, and of love, and of a sound mind." What is a sound mind? I think of someone whose thoughts are steady, secure, and anchored in faith. It gives me comfort to know that God will help us have a sound mind—that is,

He will help us turn our focus from fear to faith in His love and power. President Russell M. Nelson has said, "Faith in Jesus Christ propels us to do things we otherwise would not do. Faith that motivates us to *action* gives us more access to His power."[7] How can we act? What can we do to access God's power to make our "weak things become strong"?

Focusing on What We Can Do—the Widow's Mite

God asks that we start wherever we are and go forward from there, that we focus on what we can do instead of what we can't do. We might ask ourselves, "What can I do today with what I do know and with what capability I do have right now?"

We know the story of the poor widow who cast two mites into the temple treasury. Her offering to God was very small, but it was enough (see Mark 12:43–44). We usually think of this story of the widow's mite in terms of our monetary offerings, but it also applies to all our gifts that we can offer Heavenly Father. The widow whose love for God was stronger than her fear of not "being enough" gave her all—two little mites.

What "mites" do we have to offer? Can we, like this widow, give what we have—however seemingly little that may be—knowing our efforts are acceptable and sufficient for the Lord? Offering what we can do and what we do have is enough for the Lord to work with us and through us to bless lives. The widow focused on what she could give, not on what she couldn't. Likewise, our honest effort is all God asks for in exchange for His aid. Focusing on what we can do and showing our willingness to try is a signal to God that we are seeking His help to enhance what ability we have.

Focusing on our weaknesses blinds us to the "mites" we can offer. A daughter avoids soccer tryouts because she fears she's not good enough, but she overlooks her ability to learn fast and work hard. A young man thinks he shouldn't serve a mission because he's shy, but he overlooks his talent for loving people. A mother doesn't take a meal to a sick friend

The story of the widow and the mites shows that our efforts and offerings, no matter how small, are enough to please the Lord. Courtesy of Intellectual Reserve, Inc.

because her cooking ability is limited, but she overlooks her talent to give encouraging messages. We know that through small and simple things, great things will be brought to pass (see Alma 37:6–7). God asks us to give our best—however small and simple that may be. I can imagine a loving Heavenly Father telling us that He is pleased and thankful for every good deed we offer. He cheers for us at every attempt we make to be good and to do good.

Whatever our roles may be, we often feel stretched to the limits of our capability. The Savior invites us to walk our journey with Him by asking us to have a willing heart and a willing mind. In Exodus 35:5 we read, "Whosoever is of a willing heart, let him bring it, an offering of the Lord." We honor Christ by offering what we do have and what we can do and by being willing to trust Him and willing to try.

Willingness to Trust

In the Book of Mormon, Ammon sets a great example of trusting in the Lord's power to strengthen him. After seeing Ammon's great success in protecting King Lamoni's flocks from intruders, Ammon's friends marveled at his strength. Though in the eyes of his companions he was something of a superhero, Ammon reminded them, "I do not boast in my own strength, . . . but behold, my joy is full. . . . Yea, I know that I am nothing; as to my strength I am weak; therefore I will not boast of myself, but I will boast of my God, for in his strength I can do all things" (Alma 26:11–12). We might imagine how this story would have turned out had Ammon said at the beginning, "I've got this! Trust me! I can do it myself!" If Ammon had relied entirely on his own strength, would he have saved only part of King Lamoni's flock, cut off the arm of only a single robber, protected only a few servants? Would he have boasted of his own strength with his minimal success? Or would he have died?

Ammon's trust in God was so pure that his success in protecting the king's flocks and servants was miraculous. Ammon's story teaches a powerful lesson, linking trust in God with humility.

What is humility? Humility is often seen as a weakness, a vice instead of a virtue. In the world's eyes, to be humble is to recognize everything we don't do well or can't do at all. Is that really what the Lord intends when He asks us to be humble? In *True to the Faith* we read, "To be humble is to recognize gratefully your dependence on the Lord—to understand that you have constant need for His support. Humility is an acknowledgement that your talents and abilities are gifts from God. It is not a sign of weakness, timidity, or fear; *it is an indication that you know where your true strength lies.*"[8] I love Ammon's humility. He demonstrates the power and confidence derived from being humble.

The word *nothing* in Ammon's story is often confusing. Are we really supposed to think we are nothing? In Mosiah 4:11 we similarly read, "I would that ye should remember . . . the greatness of God, and *your own nothingness,* . . . and humble yourselves even in the depths of humility." Being *nothing* sounds contrary to the fact that God wants us to believe in our divine potential. Elder Dieter F. Uchtdorf taught, "This is a paradox of man: compared to God, man is nothing; yet we are everything to God. . . . The great deceiver knows that one of his most effective tools in leading the children of God astray is to appeal to the extremes of the paradox of man."[9] On one extreme are people who think they are *everything,* that they don't need God's power because their own ability is sufficient. On the other extreme are people who think they are *nothing,* that they are too weak to accomplish much because they are alone. Satan will do all he can to compel us to think we are everything or nothing, because his goal is to disconnect us from God—to convince us to go it alone, either in pride or despair. But Ammon teaches us that we can't go it alone. "I am nothing; as to my [own] strength I am weak" (Alma 26:12). We need God's strength. To reach our potential, we can't do it without Him!

Moses also testifies that our strength is connected to the glory, grandeur, and power of our God in Heaven. We can imagine that after Moses experienced his mighty position in Egypt and felt the praise of the world, he had a taste of thinking he was "everything." Maybe he thought he was great because of his own strength. Later he sees God face to face. He perceives the grandeur of God's creation—including him, a child of God, made in the image of heavenly parents. "Now, for this cause I know that man is *nothing*, which thing I never had supposed" (Moses 1:10; italics added). Moses learns that compared to God's power and greatness, his strength is "nothing." When Satan challenges Moses's identity, Moses replies, "I am a son of God, in the similitude of his Only Begotten" (Moses 1:13). Moses learned that he was made in the image of God, with the potential, power, and privilege to become like Him. Understanding the significance of that privilege, he knew that acquiring strength on his own was *nothing* compared to the opportunity of being empowered by God.

In other words, Satan would have us think that we are either nothing because of our own limitations or everything because of our perceptions of our own strength. Either way, we are disconnected from the power of God to help us. Therefore, when we connect ourselves to God's power, we can "boast of [our] God, for in his strength [we] can do all things" (Alma 26:12).

On my mission, Ammon's story kept me going. I too felt like I was nothing according to my own strength, and I wanted to be honest with myself about how I really felt. I didn't feel capable of doing everything that was asked of me. Self-doubt also hits me when I am trying to be a good mother. Knowing my daughters need wisdom beyond my own understanding is especially daunting. But Ammon's expression of confidence that he could do all things in the strength of the Lord continues to remind me of God's enabling power, His ability to magnify my efforts. Ammon was willing to trust. He reminds us, "I will boast of my God, for in his strength I can do all things" (verse 12). That sentence gives me hope.

Ammon knew that trusting in God's power would magnify his strength. Elder Neal A. Maxwell taught that humility involves trusting God's power:

> How can we sincerely pray to be an instrument in His hands if the instrument seeks to do the instructing? . . .
>
> If faithful, we end up acknowledging that we are in the Lord's hands and should surrender to the Lord on His terms—not ours. . . . It is only by yielding to God that we can begin to realize His will for us. And if we truly trust God, why not yield to His loving omniscience? After all, He knows us and our possibilities *much better than do we.*[10]

If God knows us and our possibilities better than we do, are we willing to trust that He knows best? Can we trust that He loves us, knows us, has our best interests at heart? Can we trust that He can make more of us than we can make of ourselves?

Trust and humility are inseparable. They complement each other and work well together. They anchor our confidence in God. Why is humility essential to accompany trust?

In the *Encyclopedia of Mormonism* we learn, "True humility is the recognition of one's imperfection that is acquired only as one joyfully, voluntarily, and *quietly submits one's whole life to God's will.*"[11] What does submission to the will of God look like? To me, it means that I trust in God's wisdom and the promptings I receive through the Spirit. It means that I trust that He knows best instead of thinking I know best. It means that I trust that He can make more of me than I can make of myself. It means that I work hard and trust that He will magnify my efforts. It means that I seek to do His will instead of wanting to do my will first. I know that humbly submitting our will to God qualifies us for the empowerment of God. "Let us glory, yea, we will glory in the Lord; yea, we will rejoice, for our joy is full; yea, we will praise our God forever. Behold, who can glory too much in the Lord? Yea, who can say too much of his great power . . . ? Behold, I say unto you, I cannot say the smallest part which I feel" (Alma 26:16).

I agree with Ammon. I cannot "glory too much in the Lord." I cannot "say too much of his great power."

Willingness to Try

The greatest problem with self-doubt is that it limits our view of who we are and what we can become. When we fear we aren't enough, we become hesitant to try, and being willing to try is the next step after learning that we must trust in the Lord. Too often we hold fast to false beliefs about ourselves and our potential. The tragedy of this mindset is captured in an empowering short story about a person observing elephants in captivity. The author (unknown) captures a false mindset of capability:

> As a man was passing the elephants [resting in their corner at a circus], he suddenly stopped, confused by the fact that these huge creatures were being held by only a small rope tied to their front leg. No chains, no cages. It was obvious that the elephants could, at any time, break away from their bonds but for some reason, they did not.
>
> He saw a trainer nearby and asked why these beautiful, magnificent animals just stood there and made no attempt to get away. "Well," [the] trainer said, "when they are very young and much smaller we use the same size rope to tie them and, at that age, it's enough to hold them. As they grow up, they are conditioned to believe they cannot break away. They believe the rope can still hold them, so they never try to break free."
>
> The man was amazed. These animals could at any time break free from their bonds but because they believed they couldn't, they were stuck right where they were.[12]

Like the elephants, how many of us go through life not willing to try because we think we don't have the ability? We may see only our limitations and weaknesses and lose sight of our possibilities. We may be unaware that our abilities have increased. We can break free of limiting beliefs! Are we willing to try?

Sometimes other people's beliefs about us affect our confidence. When my friend Sarah was in junior high school, she ran a school race for a field day. After the race, a boy said to her, "You run funny."

"Because of that comment," she told me, "I didn't sign up for another race in school. And not only did I not run races in school, but I didn't run for twenty-five years after he said that to me. I finally got over that comment from all those years ago and took up running, and I love it! Since then, I have run eleven marathons and several half marathons. As I ran the Boston Marathon at age forty-five, I thought of that boy from seventh grade, and I was proud to be a runner."

Unfortunately, the outcome of a similar experience in my life wasn't as successful. When I was in tenth grade, I sang in the a cappella choir. One day during rehearsal, a boy leaned over to me and said, "Your singing is flat." I just looked at him and said, "Oh." In my mind I was thinking, "What does that mean? I have no idea if I'm singing flat or sharp" (and honestly, I still don't have a clue). No singing career for me! After choir that year, I didn't sing in a singing group again. Today, when I sing around our home, my husband reminds me that I sing as well as he does—in a beautiful, flat monotone!

Sarah was willing to try—to put forth effort—to develop the talent of running. In contrast, I did not dedicate time to develop the talent of singing. I surrendered to doubt. It may be true that I don't have the potential to become an opera singer, but do I really have to hold myself back from being a beautiful shower singer, someone my family can listen to without covering their ears?

What limiting beliefs tie us down or hold us back? Perhaps we do indeed have the talent and capability but have let some comment or belief hold us down. Or perhaps we really don't have much singing talent but thoroughly enjoy the musical talents of others. The critical point is not letting self-doubt hold us back from becoming everything we desire to become.

Elder Holland insists that "with the gift of the Atonement of Jesus Christ and the strength of heaven to help us, we *can* improve, and the great thing about the gospel is we get credit for *trying*, even if we don't always succeed."[13] Our Lord is aware of every sincere effort we make. And each effort counts. In a BYU devotional, Cassy Budd said, "Simply showing up and starting where you are is all that can be asked of you. Regardless of your level of experience, your failures, or your perception of your own potential, wherever you are in life, you just need to show up and try."[14]

On my mission I realized that my effort was all I had to give; my effort was the invitation the Lord required so that He could step in to help. Focusing on what I *could* do instead of what I *couldn't* motivated me to give my best with whatever I had to offer.

The Lord often blesses us with what we need when we are stretched beyond our comfort zone. My twin sister shared this story from her own life:

> Many years ago, with four young children, I was faced with some challenges that would impact my marriage and my family forever. I was overwhelmed and unsure of what direction I should take and what the future looked like for me and my family. . . . For what seemed like weeks I was literally praying every few hours just to have some peace of mind and comfort and know that I could handle the challenges that lay ahead.
>
> Then, what came next was completely crazy; my bishop called and asked me if I would accept a calling to be the Relief Society pianist. I thought, "Really? I can't handle anything right now." As I laughed, I responded, "Seriously? I have not played the piano in several years and have not had a piano in my home for the last thirteen years."
>
> Undaunted, he said, "So, will you do it?" I said yes—because I was even worse at saying no than playing the piano—and returned home stunned at what I had just agreed to do.

> I spent at least twenty to thirty minutes each day practicing. About a month later, a friend called and offered to give us a piano she no longer wanted. She definitely was an answer to prayer. . . .
>
> Over the next year or two, while I served in that capacity, I realized how inspired my bishop was! I desperately needed music back in my life to give some much needed relief and solace. . . . *I noticed that while practicing the piano every day, I felt peace from the music—the peace I had asked for in so many prayers.* That experience reminded me . . . that Heavenly Father knows what each of us is going through and especially that we are not alone. Most of all I learned that Heavenly Father loves me and knows what I need to help me on this journey through life.[15]

The Lord does know us. He knows our challenges. And He knows how to minister to our needs. As we offer what we can, He blesses us in ways that we often don't know we need.

God believes in us! Can we believe in Him? Can we believe in His willingness to magnify our efforts? Can we challenge our thoughts of self-doubt and replace our fear of not being enough with thoughts that we are enough to try—that we can offer what we do have and what we can do? If we are willing to try and offer our best, the Savior will empower our efforts.

Focus on Service

As a young missionary in England, President Gordon B. Hinckley learned to put his trust in God and to focus his efforts on doing His work. He felt unsuccessful in his missionary efforts and wrote home to ask his father's advice. His father suggested that Gordon "forget [himself] and go to work."[16] That change of focus changed his mission.

Likewise, we also must forget ourselves and go to work. How do we forget ourselves when we feel inadequate? It takes humility—lots of humility! When we forget ourselves, we become more concerned about serving God than about stewing over our weaknesses; we seek to serve more than we desire to sit in self-pity. "We don't discover humility by thinking less *of* ourselves; we discover humility by thinking less *about* ourselves. . . . Humility directs our attention and love toward others and to Heavenly Father's purposes," taught Elder Uchtdorf.[17] For me, the less I worry about my abilities and the more I focus on what I can do for others, the happier I am.

Forgetting ourselves can be hard. Why? One reason is the insistent current of social messaging that encourages self-interest, self-actualization, and self-promotion. We are socialized to believe that we are the sun around which all else orbits. This attitude leads to preoccupation with ourselves instead of devotion to serving God and others. Forgetting ourselves requires a change of focus—a shift from fixating on our weaknesses to ministering to others. We choose whether we want to rely on our own strength or on the power of God. Then we go to work—with whatever ability we have at the moment.

Elder Neil L. Andersen spoke of his feelings of inadequacy as he thought about serving a mission: "I felt very inadequate and unprepared. I remember praying, 'Heavenly Father, how can I serve a mission when I know so little?' I believed in the Church, but I felt my spiritual knowledge was very limited. As I prayed, the feeling came: 'You don't know everything, but you know enough!' That reassurance gave me the courage to take the next step into the mission field."[18] Now we have over eighty thousand missionaries throughout the world who don't know everything, but they know enough—they know enough to work hard every day, to meet and serve one person at a time, and to bear witness of Christ. They offer what they have, what they know, and what they believe. It is enough.

Can we believe the Lord when He says we are enough for Him to empower us with strength to bless the lives of others? As we read in 2 Nephi 22:2, "God is my salvation; I will trust, and not be afraid; for the Lord Jehovah is my strength." The Lord empowers us not only with strength but also with the ability to bless the lives of others when we focus less on our weaknesses and more on our opportunities to humbly serve. And there is another "paradox of man": our strength increases as we strengthen others. This is the paradox at the center of Christian doctrine: "For whosoever will save his life shall lose it: and whosoever will lose his life for my sake shall find it" (Matthew 16:25).

Trusting Christ's Power—Weak Things Become Strong

From time to time, we have tasks that seem beyond our reach. Some challenges we cannot give up, we cannot change—we have to go through them. My husband encountered such a task on one portion of his trek on the Camino. Ascending the Montes de Oca on a bike, he found the climb too steep for his abilities. He rode a few meters on the rocky, muddy, narrow, and steep terrain, then pushed the bike, then carried the bike, then rode a bit more. Finally arriving at the summit, exhausted and sore, he discovered an "oasis"—a refreshment stand stocked by the locals, offering beverages and fruit for the passing pilgrims. Rested and refreshed, he continued his journey until arriving at his destination, the city of Burgos, Spain, several hours later.

When we find our tasks never-ending and overwhelming, Christ will fill in the gaps where we are weak. He will give us the strength to keep pressing forward. We trust Him. And then we keep trying. Then we find our oasis of peace—even if there is still another hill to climb. Because we know He does not doubt we can do it. Because He offers help. Because He loves us.

In giving me a difficult assignment, my mission president gave me a gift—the gift to see how the Lord views our imperfections and weaknesses and how He would like to work with us in overcoming them. I'm thankful for a mission president who taught me that the Lord knows each one of us individually. He taught me that God never doubts our potential. God believes in us. He believes in our ability to do great things even as we offer our less-than-perfect best. I realized

Photo of the rocky hill, Montes de Oca, that was overwhelming for my husband to climb on a bike—a feeling we experience with tasks that seem beyond our reach. Photo by John Rosenberg.

that I needed to change my focus to what I could do instead of what I couldn't do, to what I did know instead of what I didn't know, to the abilities I did have—however small and weak—instead of what I did not have at that moment. I learned that since God does not doubt me, I must not doubt Him.

Today I still rely on that lesson I learned on my mission. It gives me confidence as a mother, a teacher, and a wife and in my Church callings. Nephi's psalm echoes my feelings: "I know in whom I have trusted. My God hath been my support. . . . He hath filled me with his love. . . . He hath heard my cry. . . . O Lord, I have trusted in thee, and I will trust in thee forever" (2 Nephi 4:19–21, 23, 34).

President Nelson spoke of the joy we feel when we focus on Christ's power: "The gospel of Jesus Christ is filled with His power, which is available to every earnestly seeking daughter or son of God. It is my testimony that when we draw His power into our lives, both He and we will rejoice." Further, "drawing the Savior's power into our lives is to reach up to Him in faith. Such reaching requires diligent, focused effort."[19] We will experience Christ's power to make our weak things strong as we are willing to trust in Him and willing to try.

Can we recognize thoughts that are focused on fear of not being enough and change our focus to faith in the power of Christ?

Whatever our abilities may be, we often feel stretched to our limits of capability. I imagine the Savior gathering us one by one and calming our fears: "Come warm your hands by the fire of my peace and strength. I don't doubt your ability to contribute; please don't doubt my ability to strengthen you." Exodus 35:5 entreats, "Whosoever is of a willing heart, let him bring it, an offering of the Lord." We honor Christ by offering what we do have and what we can do.

Invitation: Focus on the Savior's power to strengthen you. Focus on what you can do, on what you do know, and on what you do have. Offer your best—it is enough for Him to make weak things strong.

Think-in-ink journal challenge: Make a list of the "mites" you have to offer. (Who can you bless with your "mites"?) Write down one weakness you would like the Lord to help you with. Write down what you could do to try to overcome that weakness with the ability you have at this moment. Ask the Lord to empower your efforts.

Notes

1. Dan Baker and Cameron Stauth, *What Happy People Know: How the New Science of Happiness Can Change Your Life for the Better* (New York: St. Martin's Griffin, 2003), 24, 72; italics in the original.
2. Sebastian Kipman, "15 Highly Successful People Who Failed on Their Way to Success," Lifehack, updated March 2, 2021, https://www.lifehack.org/articles/productivity/15-highly-successful-people-who-failed-their-way-success.html.
3. Thomas S. Monson, "Doubt Not, Fear Not" (commencement address, Brigham Young University, Provo, UT, April 24, 2003).
4. Kevin J Worthen, "Fear Not" (Brigham Young University devotional, September 12, 2017), 2–3, speeches.byu.edu.
5. Dieter F. Uchtdorf, "Perfect Love Casteth Out Fear," *Ensign*, May 2017, 106–7.
6. Baker and Stauth, *What Happy People Know*, 80, 107–8.
7. Russell M. Nelson, "Drawing the Power of Jesus Christ into Our Lives," *Ensign*, May 2017, 41; italics added.
8. *True to the Faith: A Gospel Reference* (Salt Lake City: The Church of Jesus Christ of Latter-day Saints, 2004), 86; italics added. See also John 5:30.
9. Dieter F. Uchtdorf, "You Matter to Him," *Ensign*, November 2011, 20; italics added.
10. Neal A. Maxwell, "Willing to Submit," *Ensign*, May 1985, 71–72; italics added.
11. Alice T. Clark, "Humility," in *Encyclopedia of Mormonism*, ed. Daniel H. Ludlow (New York: Macmillan, 1992), 1:663; italics added.
12. Thanh_min, "The Elephant Rope," Medium, April 8, 2017, https://medium.com/motivationapp/the-elephant-rope-c22ee790a226.
13. Jeffrey R. Holland, "Tomorrow the Lord Will Do Wonders among You," *Ensign*, May 2016, 125–26.
14. Cassy Budd, "On Failing and Finishing" (Brigham Young University devotional, February 14, 2017), 3, speeches.byu.edu.
15. Maylarie Ostler, email message to author, February 20, 2020; italics added.
16. Quoted in Sheri L. Dew, *Go Forward with Faith: The Biography of Gordon B. Hinckley* (Salt Lake City: Deseret Book, 1996), 64.

17. Dieter F. Uchtdorf, "Pride and the Priesthood," *Ensign*, November 2010, 58.
18. Neil L. Andersen, "You Know Enough," *Ensign*, November 2008, 13.
19. Nelson, "Drawing the Power of Jesus Christ," 42, 41.

chapter four

FOCUS ON HIS GIFTS TO US

Feelings of self-doubt come from comparing our weaknesses to others' strengths. The Savior helps us enhance the gifts and talents He has given us. We can change our focus to enhancing strengths instead of dwelling on weaknesses—focusing on what we have instead of what we don't have. We can focus on developing our own abilities instead of comparing our abilities.

National Football League (NFL) quarterback Steve Young shared a story about the danger of comparing ourselves to others. As he sat next to Stephen R. Covey on an airplane one day, Young discussed his experience playing for the San Francisco 49ers. He shared his feelings of inadequacy playing backup quarterback to the very talented Joe Montana. He felt that the comparisons between him and Montana made it impossible to be successful. Covey asked him if he was fortunate enough to get advice from Montana and the coaches that could help him improve. Young assured him that the best resources in the league were at his disposal. According to Young, the conversation between him and Stephen Covey went as follows:

> "If I understand your situation with the 49ers correctly," he continued, "you are in the one place in the NFL where you can find out just how good you can get."
>
> Now he really had my attention. . . .
>
> "So here's the question," he said. "Do you want to find out how good you can get?"
>
> "Yeah, I do."
>
> "I mean, some people are just afraid to find out," he said.
>
> "No. I absolutely want to find out."
>
> "Then go do it," he said. "Good luck."
>
> . . . It was divine intervention that forced me to rethink my situation in a completely different paradigm.
>
> *I have a quest*, I told myself. *My quest is to find out how good I can become.*
>
> *It's not about comparisons or outside expectations.*
>
> It wasn't going to be easy. But I couldn't wait to get back on the field.[1]

Young went on to become a successful quarterback, including winning the Most Valuable Player award when his team won Super Bowl XXIX in 1995.

Are we willing to see how good we can get? Sometimes we are afraid to see how good we may become. We fear not measuring up. We fear judgment and criticism from others. We fear we will let others down, let ourselves down, or worse, let God down. The words of President Thomas S. Monson encourage us: "My young brothers and sisters, don't take counsel of your fears. Don't say to yourselves, 'I'm not wise enough . . . so I shall choose the easier way.' I plead with you to tax your talent, and our Heavenly Father will make you equal to those decisions."[2] How do we tax our talents? What gets in our way? Fear can prevent us from using the gifts and talents we have been given. And this kind of fear is most paralyzing when we compare ourselves to others.

Comparing ourselves to others happens all too often. We feel weak because we see the strengths in others that we lack. Yet we need to learn and grow from each other. About the people of his day, the Apostle Paul warned, "They measuring themselves by themselves, and comparing themselves among themselves, are not wise" (2 Corinthians 10:12). How do we learn from others in a way that motivates and inspires us to become our best selves without becoming discouraged by comparing our weaknesses to another's strengths?

The Problem with Comparisons

We see gifts and talents in people all around us, and we may desire to emulate others' abilities. It is easy to compare ourselves to others. Comparisons are a challenge I face when teaching at the university. In the company of excellent professors, it is easy to feel inadequate. It's also easy for me to feel inadequate when I compare my physical fitness to that of other women in my ward. Many are thin and physically fit and run marathons. Me? I'm lucky to walk around our neighborhood, and I'm thrilled if I actually exercise five days in a week. (Exercising daily has been a New Year's resolution of mine for at least the last thirty years of my life—and I'm still working on it!)

Comparisons often distort reality. This happens frequently when viewing social media. While scrolling through our feed, we may think, "Kate is a gourmet cook and an immaculate housekeeper; my husband does his own laundry and is lucky to get a bowl of soup." But in reality, Kate has probably burned a lot of dinners too! Or "On Anne's Facebook page, her ten beautiful children are the picture of perfection, while we wake up at ten o'clock in the morning and hang out in our pajamas all day." But Anne probably has kids that scream at each other too!

Regarding these types of thoughts, Elder Dieter F. Uchtdorf reminded us, "God is fully aware that you and I are not perfect. Let me add: God is also fully aware that the people you think are perfect are not. And yet we spend so much time and energy comparing ourselves to others—usually comparing our weaknesses to their strengths. This drives us to create expectations for ourselves that are impossible to meet. As a result, we never celebrate our good efforts because they seem to be less than what someone else does."[3] Are we hesitant to develop our talents and abilities because we think our efforts will not be as good as someone else's?

Comparisons create unneeded stress from unhealthy competition. Instead of competing with ourselves, we compete against each other, chasing the expectations for another person instead of creating our own. BYU religion professor J. B. Haws spoke of the self-obsessed nature of making comparisons:

> Think of all of the questions that bombard us on a daily basis: Did I get picked for a leadership position on my mission? Did I score more points than my rival in the basketball game? Did I get the highest score on the test in my class? Was I the one student from BYU who landed the internship? Did I play more flawlessly in my audition than did everyone else? Did my witty comment in Sunday School make more people laugh than my roommate's comment did? If I glance over at the treadmill next to mine, will I find that I am running at a faster pace? And on and on and on.

> These constantly nipping questions are all about me, me, me. And it is exhausting.
>
> Doesn't it sound freeing and liberating to think less about ourselves?[4]

Can we see how good we can become—not compared to others, but compared to our personal best?

Comparisons also inhibit relationships. While serving as Relief Society General President, Elaine L. Jack said, "Comparisons may keep you from achieving your potential and basking in associations that will enrich your lives and the lives of others."[5] Are we more focused on comparing ourselves to others than on connecting with others? When we compare, we hesitate to share what we have, thinking that we don't have much to offer, so we don't extend ourselves to uplift and bless others. We lose out on relationships because comparisons hold us back from interacting. When we focus on what we don't have compared to others, we become too preoccupied with ourselves to forget ourselves and to focus on what we have to bless other lives.

Comparisons smother personal joy. Comparing drives out the happiness we can find in what we do have and what we can do. Elder Quentin L. Cook said, "We cannot be grateful and envious at the same time. If we truly want to have the Spirit of the Lord and experience joy and happiness, we should rejoice in our blessings and be grateful."[6] Gratitude withers on the vine of comparison. We look for what we don't have instead of what we do have.

Comparisons also blind us to the gifts and talents God has given us—however big or small they may seem. I think this is what the Savior meant when He said, "But with some I am not well pleased, for they will not open their mouths, but they hide the talent which I have given unto them, because of the fear of man. Wo unto such, for mine anger is kindled against them. . . . Thou [shalt not] bury thy talent that it may not be known" (Doctrine and Covenants 60:2, 13).

We will never stop competing and comparing our abilities until we discover and develop our own abilities.

Parable of the Talents

The Savior taught us about faithful stewardship over what we have been given. In the parable of the talents, the Lord likened the kingdom of heaven to "a man travelling into a far country, who called his own servants, and delivered unto them his goods. And unto one he gave five talents, to another two, and to another one; to every man according to his several ability; and straightway took his journey" (Matthew 25:14–15). We know that the servant with five talents worked to gain five more and that the servant with two talents worked to gain two more, but the servant with one talent buried it and was left with nothing.

To the servants who worked hard to gain more talents, the man replied, "Well done, thou good and faithful servant: thou hast been faithful over a few things, I will make thee ruler over many things: enter thou into the joy of thy lord" (verse 21; see also verse 23). The Lord was pleased with the servants' diligence in using the talents they had been given and earning even more. And He gave each servant the same reward, regardless of how many talents he was given. However, the Lord was not pleased with the "slothful servant" (verse 26) who buried and neglected his talent. To that servant He said, "Take therefore the talent from him, and give it unto him which hath ten talents. For unto every one that hath shall be given, and he shall have abundance: but from him that hath not shall be taken away even that which he hath" (verses 28–29).

This parable refers to a talent (a coin), which was a very large sum of money in Roman times. We can learn financial-management principles from this story. But the Savior is not interested in stock markets; He is interested in stewardship. The point of the parable is to be grateful and faithful with what we have been given—which applies to our skills and gifts. And we too will receive the same eternal reward as wise stewards, regardless of how many talents we were initially given.

Some have received many talents, others few. We don't know why God gives others talents and abilities that we don't possess. But we do know that the Lord wants us to use and develop what we have been given. Elder Bruce R. McConkie taught, "Every man must use such talents as he may have or they will be lost. If a man cannot compose music, perhaps he can sing in the choir; if he cannot write books, at least he can read them; if he cannot paint pictures, he can learn to appreciate the artistry of others; if he cannot achieve preeminence in one specific field, so be it, he still can succeed in his own field; for each man has some talent, and he will be judged on the basis of how he uses what he has."[7]

What happened to the slothful servant? He buried the one talent he had been given. Why? Was he afraid of losing it? Did he not recognize the value of his gift? Did self-doubt and fear of failure prevent him from using his one talent? Perhaps his doubt increased as he watched the other servants multiply their talents. We may not know the answers to these questions, but we know that he held himself back from earning more. Do we ever feel like this servant? Do we try to develop our talents, or do we hide them because we feel they might not be as great as others' talents?

Since Christ invites us to become at one ("at-one") with Him, He knows we must obtain talents, gifts, and abilities to become like Him. Do we recognize what gifts He has already granted us? Are we great receivers of those gifts? Elder Uchtdorf reminds us:

> In our day the Savior has said that those "who [receive] all things with thankfulness shall be made glorious" [Doctrine and Covenants 78:19], and "the fulness of the earth is [theirs]" [see Doctrine and Covenants 59:15–21]. . . .
>
> . . . Do we feel our Father's love expressed in these gifts? Do we receive them in a way that deepens our relationship with this wonderful, divine Giver? Or are we too distracted to even notice what God gives us each and every day?
>
> We know that "God loveth a cheerful giver" [2 Corinthians 9:7], but does He not also love a good, grateful, and cheerful receiver?[8]

Our task is to recognize and develop the gifts we have been given. The Savior promises to enhance our talents and gifts when we choose to act. Where do we start? What can we do to recognize and enhance the gifts and talents God has given us?

Finding Our Strengths

When I asked friends what helped them recognize and develop their talents, several of them responded the same way: "What talents?" "I don't really have any talents." I can relate. I've never considered myself very talented. I'm not musical or athletic, and I'm not a "Star Baker"—all talents I'm still determined to acquire someday! (I'm hoping this happens before I die, but if not, they will still be on my list for the next life.) One friend shared this experience: "When I was a teenager, I used to say to my mom, 'I don't have any talents; I'm not a great singer, dancer, musician, or athlete.' Her response was always the same: 'But you are great at organizing.' Organizing? What teenager wants to be great at organizing? Well, in the last thirty years of my life, that strength has been such a gift to me in many ways. I wish I could go back to my teenage self and say, 'Just wait! You will be so grateful for this talent!'"

Ralph Waldo Emerson encouraged us to find our strengths: "You are sensitive to a thousand influences . . . instructed by the past . . . invited by the future. You are not born equal—you are born unique. You have powers that have come to you from a host of ancestors. Your strengths are greater than your weaknesses. Finding our strengths, our unique powers, should be a purpose of the journey of life."[9] I love the idea that a host of ancestors is strengthening us. Sometimes we obtain talents by learning from good examples, inherit natural talent, or both. Have you inherited the ability to be kind and compassionate from Grandmother Betty? Are you musically talented like Grandpa Marvin? Are you good at fixing things like your father? Or have you had an easy time learning academically like your mother?

We have help from both sides of the veil encouraging us to discover and use the gifts and talents God has given us to build His kingdom. I imagine that this host of ancestors is "round about [us], to bear [us] up" (Doctrine and Covenants 84:88), reminding us that our strengths are greater than our weaknesses. Every talent, every gift is needed! God needs us to discover our gifts, talents, and strengths and use them for the good of others and ourselves.

What can we do to recognize the gifts and talents God has given us? Some gifts and talents that are commonly seen as the most important are intelligence, wealth, power, position, appearance, and performance skills (musical, athletic, and artistic). Yet we look over other gifts that are just as important—or more important—and highly beneficial. Elder Marvin J. Ashton describes these gifts that are not always recognized:

> Among these may be your gifts—gifts not so evident but nevertheless real and valuable . . . : the gift of asking; the gift of listening; the gift of hearing and using a still, small voice; the gift of being able to weep; the gift of avoiding contention; the gift of being agreeable; the gift of avoiding vain repetition; the gift of seeking that which is righteous; the gift of not passing judgment; the gift of looking to God for guidance; the gift of being a disciple; the gift of caring for others; the gift of being able to ponder; the gift of offering prayer; the gift of bearing a mighty testimony; and the gift of receiving the Holy Ghost.[10]

Many gifts from God are unseen: gifts of the Spirit, gifts of character, and gifts of godly attributes. As we learn in Doctrine and Covenants 46:16–26, "All these gifts come from God, for the benefit of the children of God." When we dig deep to recognize gifts from God, let's not forget those of a more spiritual and invisible nature. I admire the talent one friend has for patience, another for selfless service, another for a happy disposition, another for creativity, another for wisdom and insight. There is so much talent around us!

Writing about talents in a journal can be helpful: identify what skills come easily to you and what skills you've gained only by hard work. What abilities have others seen in you? Often we recognize our talents by the gracious and encouraging words of others who point out our talents to us. I'll never forget my Young Women leader Sally Todd, who gave me a mirror that had writing all around the border of the frame. She had written a list of talents she saw in me. I remember looking at the mirror and thinking, "Really? I have those abilities? Is it true?" Her kind encouragement helped me consider the blessings and abilities God has given me.

If we have received a patriarchal blessing, it can be helpful to study it, looking for gifts God has blessed us with. We can look for sentences—or impressions that come to mind—about gifts, talents, and abilities we have been given to build up the kingdom of God on earth. They can often remind us that God loves us, is mindful of us, and has marvelous things in store for us.

Psychologist Dan Baker realized that helping people find their strengths was an important key to overcoming self-doubt. He discovered, "When I could help people to find their strengths, they didn't need to go to war against their weakness." He shared the importance of enhancing strengths in his work helping girls with eating disorders: "I knew better than to confront their weaknesses. I never talked about eating with them. They weren't good at eating. I talked about what they *were* good at and about what they loved. Then, when they finally found their strengths, they began to nourish their newfound selves. . . . Focusing on strengths works simply because it feels better than focusing on weakness. It creates energy, which is always necessary for transformation."[11] Baker learned that dwelling on weaknesses is a waste of energy—energy that's needed to achieve healing and change.

Remember what my daughter's teacher told me: "Whatever you focus on will increase." If we continue to focus on our weaknesses, our self-doubt will increase. If we focus on enhancing our talents and strengths, our abilities will increase. Going to war against our weaknesses is not the solution for overcoming our feelings of inadequacy. Focusing on what we have is always more productive than focusing on what we don't have. With this in mind, how can we develop the talents that we do have?

Developing Gifts and Talents

In Doctrine and Covenants 6:33 we read, "Fear not to do good, . . . for whatsoever ye sow, that shall ye also reap; therefore, if ye sow good ye shall also reap good for your reward." Building talents begins with our thoughts and actions. We learn from Charles A. Hall, "We sow our thoughts, and we reap our actions; we sow our actions, and we reap our habits; we sow our habits, and we reap our characters; we sow our characters, and we reap our destiny."[12] With these words in mind, I would like to highlight three things we can do to develop our gifts and talents: prepare our mindset, learn from others, and work hard.

Prepare our mindset

How can we prepare our thoughts to magnify our strengths? How do we talk to ourselves? Statements such as "That's just the way I am," "I can't change," and "There is nothing I can do about it" imply that we have no ability to change or grow. But we do! That is the point of God's plan for progression—we can grow, we can change, and we can become better all the time. We are made in God's image with divine potential to continually develop more talents and abilities. We must keep changing and growing to become godlike.

Changing our focus from a "fixed mindset" to a "growth mindset" enhances our talents. As we discussed in chapter 1, psychologist Carol Dweck describes a fixed mindset as closed to change, whereas a growth mindset is open to learning and growing.[13] Someone with a fixed mindset thinks, "I am who I am, and I can't do anything about it. I have little ability to change and improve." For example, Ashley says, "I have no musical or athletic ability, so there is no use in trying to develop those talents. I have to settle for the way I am." Kayla says, "I'm not smart and never will be. I can't do anything about it."

In contrast, a person with a growth mindset thinks, "I have agency and the ability to learn, grow, and develop my abilities. I can work hard and acquire new strength." People with a growth mindset don't just seek challenge, they thrive on it. They want to become better. They are on a quest to see how good they can get, just as Steve Young was. We can shift our thoughts from "I'm not a great communicator" to "I can learn to become a great communicator. I'm going to do everything I can to be a better listener and responder." Or "I can't play the guitar yet, but I'm excited to take lessons and practice every day." Or "I need help to control my temper. I know it's going to be hard, but I believe it's possible. I'll keep trying until patience becomes a hallmark of my character!"

Dweck encourages us to open our minds to growth opportunities. We see life differently when we see the possibility of growth instead of dwelling on the false idea that we will be stuck where we are forever—as if we can't do anything about it.

What talents would we like to develop? Can we look for possibilities with a growth mindset?

In a BYU devotional, sports psychologist Craig Manning emphasized the need for a proactive mindset in developing talents and abilities. He shared this story from when he played tennis for a college team:

> When I was a student at BYU, I realized that I needed to think more positively. I started working on this, and every time I caught myself thinking or talking to myself in negative, reactive ways, saying, "Your backhand stinks" or "Don't miss that backhand," I would stop that thought and immediately replace it with thoughts such as "I love my backhand" or "I am going to rip it down the line." And instead of saying to myself, "School is tough; BYU is too hard for me," I started telling myself, "I've got this; I can get good grades." At some point I realized that I would always say to myself, "Don't forget this" or "You'd better not forget this for the

> exam," so one of my favorite phrases became "I will remember this." . . .
>
> What is potentially the greatest lesson the Lord has taught me is that faith begins with how you talk to yourself.[14]

I love how Manning learned that "faith begins with how you talk to yourself." How do we talk to ourselves about our abilities? Do our thoughts show our trust in and gratitude for God's promise that we are capable of growth? Do we have faith in His ability to help us? Do we believe we are endowed with agency—the ability to act? If we believe in what the Lord makes possible for us, we will talk to ourselves differently. We will catch ourselves in negative thoughts and choose more productive thoughts. Manning learned to prepare his mind ahead of time to think of positive, proactive, short phrases during potentially stressful times. He chose where to focus his thoughts, and this directed his actions.

Our thoughts guide our behavior. How many of us have set a goal not to eat sugar, then noticed over the following week that instead of eating less sugar we ate much more sugar? That's because we told our brain what not to do but didn't tell it what to do. If we want to reinforce a particular positive behavior, we have to state the positive behavior we want our brain to think about. The key is focusing on what *to do*, not on what *not to do*. What is within our ability right now? What action can we take? We can decrease doubtful thoughts about our abilities by preparing our minds with positive thoughts to focus on instead.

In a July 2020 fireside, Manning challenged members of my stake to create habits for proactive thinking patterns. He taught a principle called the "3 to 1 ratio": it takes three positive thoughts to counteract the impact of one negative thought. Or, for every *reactive* thought that is full of self-doubt and fear, it takes three *proactive* thoughts to counteract the reactive thought—and the negative impact. He encouraged us to focus on what we can do instead of what we can't do by doing the following:

- *Start every morning with three "can-do" statements*, such as "I will _____," "I can _____," and "I am capable of _____." By doing this, we train our conscious brains to focus and spend time on what we can do.
- *Create a power statement to replace a thought filled with self-doubt.* Prepare a short phrase or a couple of words to think of every time a doubtful thought creeps into your mind. For example, you could say, "I've got this," "I can do this," or "God believes in me." We can quickly transform a thought that reflects insecurity, doubt, or fear into a positive thought with a power statement of capability.
- *Write down the answers to these questions: What are three things I'm doing well? What is one thing I could improve?* Answering these questions will keep our thoughts at a 3 to 1 ratio—for every one behavior we want to improve, we focus on three behaviors that we're doing well. The point is to turn our focus on our strengths and build on them while acknowledging where we need to improve to enhance our progress.[15]

We make more progress by enhancing our strengths than by dwelling on our weaknesses. How can we prepare our thoughts to enhance our abilities when we play a sport, make a dinner, help a child, perform in church, or take on new responsibilities at work? We can focus our thoughts on what we can do with the talent and ability we already have. For example, we can change the thought "I'm a terrible cook" to "I love pasta, and I can make a great sauce with killer zucchini noodles." "I'm not talented" can become "God has given me the gift to think of others' feelings. I'm going to brighten someone's day today." "I'm going to be a failure at my new job" can become "I'm brand-new at this job and have lots to learn, but I can work hard and learn from everyone around me."

Preparing our minds by focusing on what we can do instead of what we can't do is a powerful habit that helps us enhance our talents and abilities.

Learn from others

It's also essential to develop our talents by learning from others' strengths. Our daughter Eliza was a competitive gymnast for several years. Gymnastics is a very demanding sport. She spent hours after school working out with her team. And we spent hours and days driving back and forth from the gym, going to meets, and watching her practice. During one week of practice, Eliza had just mastered the difficult skills of a back handspring on the balance beam and a kip cast to handstand on the uneven bars when I approached her coach and asked when she could move up to the next level of competition. The coach looked at me and said, "That will depend entirely upon how well she listens and applies the corrections we give her." Her coach didn't point out Eliza's flaws. She didn't praise her talent. She spoke about her ability to be humble. The key to Eliza's growth was her willingness to learn from her coaches. Her coaches were not shy in giving corrections, because they wanted to keep her safe from injury and help her master skills. Eliza's success would be determined by how well she would listen to and apply the suggestions given to her by those who had greater expertise in her sport.

Throughout our lives, we need coaches who can offer corrections for improvement. And we need to be safe. We advance to new levels of refinement when we seek suggestions. Are we willing to listen to and learn from others to help ourselves progress?

Steve Young went from feeling threatened by Joe Montana to feeling excited to learn from him. Montana's gifts were an asset for Young, not an obstacle. Can we look at others' talents as gifts that we can learn from instead of looking at them as points of comparison designed to make us feel weak?

Are we on a quest to see how good we can get, enhancing our talents by learning from others' strengths? Having an open heart and mind and recognizing that we can learn from one another is essential. We can be happy for others and their strengths and feel grateful that we can learn from them. There is so much goodness and talent around us to learn from.

As we develop our talents, we need to beware of pride. My friend's daughter learned this difficult lesson when she played on a high school soccer team. She was one of the best players on the team. Her coaches had high expectations for her until she reached her junior year in high school, when they recognized a problem. The coaches told this player's mother that she was not coachable. She wasn't willing to accept suggestions for improvement. Unfortunately, she was cut from the team. Pride got in the way of developing her talent.

President Dallin H. Oaks has taught, "[Pride] is an attitude that commences with personal comparisons with others and leads to demeaning thoughts or oppressive actions. . . . The pride of self-satisfaction imposes its primary effects upon the one who is proud. His attitude blocks his own progress."[16] Can we look at our own behavior and see if pride is blocking our progress? Are we losing out on growth and development because of our lack of humility?

Most of us don't consider ourselves prideful if we are the ones who lack a talent and envy the one who has it. After all, that person has the talent and we don't, so doesn't that give us a right to tear that person down to make ourselves feel better? And why is it prideful to look for the negative in someone who has what we desire? We think, "I'm not hurting her; I'm just trying to find weaknesses in her to make myself feel better"—as if we are seeking some kind of confirmation that she isn't perfect. If our identity is centered on how we compare to those around us, we will always battle pride.

Pride feeds on comparisons. A proud person thinks he or she is better than others. Pride also involves a destructive pattern of criticizing and demeaning others to exalt oneself. We fail to appreciate others' strengths because we want to see weakness. Pride feeds on our desire to make others look bad so we can feel better about who we are or what we have done. And it prevents us from appreciating the goodness we can learn from others, because we are too focused on ourselves. C. S. Lewis has written, "Pride gets no pleasure out of having something, only out of having more of it than the next man. . . . It is the comparison that makes you proud: the pleasure of being above the rest. Once the element of competition has gone, pride has gone."[17]

The antidote for pride is humility. If Kate feels bad that she can't play the violin as well as Sarah, she can take violin lessons to improve her talent, and she can appreciate and learn from Sarah's talent. If Robert is embarrassed that he failed a chemistry test, he can ask classmates who did well on the exam for study suggestions and seek his teacher's advice for improvement. If we are on a quest to see how good we can become, humility is essential. A humble person seeks to learn from others. "An emotionally healthy person will make a plan to take herself/himself from the reality of where he/she is to a higher and better self," said counselor John Lund.[18]

Learning from others is essential for developing talents. Can we focus less on comparing our talents to others' talents and focus more on appreciating and learning from them?

Work hard

Developing talents requires hard work. My daughter's coach told her, "Hard work beats talent when talent doesn't work hard." Some people have natural talent, but that doesn't mean those without natural talent can't become good with discipline and effort. Many of us have had to work our way through school without natural talent or work hard at homemaking skills that don't come naturally. We can all learn and develop skills, no matter the lack of natural gifts.

A friend told me she learned how to develop talents by serving in the Church. She didn't know what she could do until she was asked to accept a calling outside her comfort zone. It challenged her to develop new skills of public speaking, teaching, leading a group of youth, and conducting music. Often we don't know what gifts and talents we have until we try something new and stretch our capability.

Learning how to work hard and not give up when the going gets tough is essential. My husband's mother taught him the value of hard work when he was a young boy. One Saturday she asked him to sweep the garage. When he had finished sweeping, she told him that he needed to sweep the garage again because it was still dirty. "You missed the corners," she said. He finished again, and his mother was still not satisfied.

"Do I really have to do it again?" he asked.

"Yes, again," she responded. And again. And again. She made him sweep the floor six times before it looked clean to her. My husband said that that experience taught him to work hard not only at completing a task but at doing it well and thoroughly. His acquired talent for detail and hard work has been a significant blessing throughout his life. He learned that if a task is worth doing, it's worth doing well.

Developing talents takes time. It takes hard work. Doctrine and Covenants 60:13 says, "Thou shalt not idle away thy time, neither shalt thou bury thy talent that it may not be known." Enhancing talents always requires diligence and endurance, even if we have to sweep the garage six times! When we learn how to work hard at our day-to-day tasks, we learn how to work hard spiritually. Discipline, consistency, perseverance, patience, and hope are all essential lessons that will help us work hard in spiritual endeavors such as seeking personal revelation (which requires a lot of hard work!) and creating strong gospel study habits. Elder Neal A. Maxwell taught, "The capacity to work and work wisely will never become obsolete. . . . I have not seen any perspiration-free shortcuts to the celestial kingdom; there is no easy escalator to take us there."[19] So the next time you have a child who whines that he has to clean out the garage, you can remind him, "You're learning how to work hard because there is no escalator to celestial glory." We work hard because it's working through weaknesses that refines us and helps us become like Christ.

God needs us to discover our gifts, talents, and strengths and to use them for good. We need one another. We grow together. We can learn from the goodness, strength, and talent around us. When we are on a quest to see how good we can become, it is enough for the Lord to work with us and through us to bless lives around us.

Sharing Our Gifts and Talents

On the Camino, we could see the talents in our students, each one contributing to the success of the group. Some students had the talent of encouraging others; others were fun and witty; others were helpful and thoughtful; and others were punctual and reliable. One of the talents the members of our group shared that blessed my life and the lives of hundreds of strangers was singing. On several occasions, the students sang in the small Romanesque churches after a service for pilgrims. Sometimes they sang standing; other times they sang sitting in a circle. A handful of pilgrims would usually gather to listen. Then more would congregate. And more and more. Our students sang Latter-day Saint hymns to pilgrims from several countries. These hymns were often unknown to the other pilgrims, but the Spirit was tangible. "Be Still, My Soul," "Abide with Me," and "I Stand All Amazed" were some of the group's favorites. The four-part harmony, the sincerity of the words, and the unity and love in the group all contributed to these spiritually touching performances. One pilgrim from another Christian faith thanked our students and said, "Oh, thank you so much. I've always wanted to hear the Mormon Tabernacle Choir! It

Photo of Camino study abroad group sharing their talent of singing in a church. Photo by author.

was so nice to hear you." A minor correction was needed! Needless to say, people appreciated fifteen BYU students sharing their singing talent that day!

We read in Matthew 5:15–16, "Neither do men light a candle, and put it under a bushel, but on a candlestick; and it giveth light unto all that are in the house. Let your light so shine before men, that they may see your good works, and glorify your Father which is in heaven." Can we share the light God has given us? Are we willing to do so? Can we pull our gifts and talents out from under the bushel?

President David O. McKay shared what he thought the Savior might ask us about our stewardships in this life. The first three questions he proposed were the following: "First, He will request an accountability report about your relationship with your wife [or husband]. . . . Second, He will want an accountability report about each of your children individually. . . . Third, He will want to know what you personally have done with the talents you were given in the pre-existence."[20] Can we be wise stewards over what we have been given? Can we focus on what we have instead of on what we don't have?

When we are on a quest to see how good we may become, we develop skills, knowledge, and wisdom to bless the lives of others. We develop our talents by preparing our minds with a growth mindset, we learn from others' strengths, and we work hard. While speaking to a group of Relief Society sisters, President Eliza R. Snow urged, "My sisters, let us cultivate ourselves, that we may be capable of doing much good."[21] We need each other. We are fed and taught by the goodness we see in each other.

When we share the gifts and talents we have been given, we become powerful instruments in God's hands to help build His kingdom. We will experience joy and fulfillment and bless lives around us. I'm so thankful for the goodness and talents of others around me that have blessed my life. They motivate me to do better and be better.

Focusing on what we have instead of what we don't have is empowering. Elder Bruce R. McConkie taught, "I start where I am, and I go forward from there. I start using such talent as I have, and I begin to apply principles of eternal truth to my life. And I consult and counsel with the Lord in the process. And no matter where I am, the gospel takes me forward and onward and upward, and blessings flow to me that will ennoble and sanctify and improve me in this life and eventually give me glory and honor and dignity in the life to come."[22]

I imagine the Savior walking beside us to offer support, saying, "Look at what you have been given! You have so much to contribute for good. You have been given talents and blessings to make your life joyful, fulfilling, and meaningful. Please recognize them, appreciate them, use them, and share them! Let your light shine that it may glorify our Father."

Invitation: Focus on recognizing and enhancing the talents and gifts God has given you. Focus on what you have instead of on what you don't have. Finally, focus on developing your own abilities instead of comparing your abilities.

Think-in-ink journal challenge: Write down three gifts and talents God has given you. (Are they visible or less visible talents?) Write down one talent you would like to develop. When and how can you work on this talent? Who can you learn from?

Notes

1. "Steve Young: On Faith, Family, and Football," *LDS Living*, September/October 2016, 32; adapted from Steve Young and Jeff Benedict, *QB: My Life behind the Spiral* (Boston: Houghton Mifflin Harcourt, 2016).
2. Thomas S. Monson, "Life's Greatest Decisions" (Brigham Young University devotional, September 7, 2003), speeches.byu.edu.
3. Dieter F. Uchtdorf, "Forget Me Not," *Ensign*, November 2011, 120.
4. J. B. Haws, "Wrestling with Comparisons" (Brigham Young University devotional, May 7, 2019), 6–7, speeches.byu.edu.
5. Elaine L. Jack, "These Things Are Manifested unto Us Plainly," *Ensign*, November 1990, 89.
6. Quentin L. Cook, "Rejoice!," *Ensign*, November 1996, 30.
7. Bruce R. McConkie, *Doctrinal New Testament Commentary*, vol. 1, *The Gospels* (Salt Lake City: Bookcraft, 1976), 689.
8. Dieter F. Uchtdorf, "The Good and Grateful Receiver" (First Presidency Christmas devotional, December 2, 2012), broadcasts.ChurchofJesusChrist.org.
9. Ralph Waldo Emerson, quoted in Thomas S. Monson, "Guideposts for Life's Journey" (Brigham Young University–Idaho commencement address, August 22, 2003), https://byui.edu/devotionals/president-thomas-s-monson-summer-2003.
10. Marvin J. Ashton, "There Are Many Gifts," *Ensign*, November 1987, 20.
11. Dan Baker and Cameron Stauth, *What Happy People Know: How the New Science of Happiness Can Change Your Life for the Better* (New York: St. Martin's Griffin, 2003), 73–76.
12. Charles A. Hall, in *Home Book of Quotations*, sel. Burton Stevenson (New York: Dodd, Mead, 1935), 845; quoted in Delbert L. Stapley, "Good Habits Develop Good Character," *Ensign*, November 1974, 20.
13. See Carol Dweck, *Mindset: The New Psychology of Success* (New York: Ballantine Books, 2016), 12–13.
14. Craig Manning, "The Power of Your Words" (Brigham Young University devotional, January 31, 2017), 4, speeches.byu.edu.

15. Craig Manning, "How to Not Only Survive, but Thrive during the Challenging Times We're Living in," fireside, Lindon Utah Stake, July 26, 2020, https://youtu.be/q99tVntkqzs.
16. Dallin H. Oaks, *Pure in Heart* (Salt Lake City: Bookcraft, 1988), 96.
17. C. S. Lewis, *Mere Christianity* (New York: Macmillan, 1952), 109–10.
18. John Lewis Lund, *How to Hug a Porcupine: Dealing with Toxic and Difficult to Love Personalities* (n.p.: Communications Company, 1999), 278.
19. Neal A. Maxwell, "Put Your Shoulder to the Wheel," *Ensign*, May 1998, 38–39.
20. David O. McKay, from notes of Fred A. Baker, Managing Director, Department of Physical Facilities; quoted in Robert D. Hales, "Understandings of the Heart" (Brigham Young University devotional, March 15, 1988), 8, speeches.byu.edu.
21. Eliza R. Snow, "Let Us Cultivate Ourselves," address, Salt Lake City Seventeenth Ward Union Hall, Salt Lake City, Utah Territory, February 18, 1869. Reprinted in Jennifer Reeder and Kate Holbrook, eds., *At the Pulpit: 185 Years of Discourses by Latter-day Saint Women* (Salt Lake City: Deseret Book, 2017), 42.
22. Bruce R. McConkie, "Agency or Inspiration—Which?" (Brigham Young University devotional, February 27, 1973), 6, speeches.byu.edu.

chapter five

FOCUS ON HIS VOICE

Feelings of self-doubt come when we try to do too many things at once. The Savior can provide guidance about what to do with our time and energy so that we don't feel overwhelmed. We can focus on listening to His voice, felt through the Holy Spirit, to discern what is most needful.

In his painting *The Burden of the Responsible Man*, James C. Christensen portrays the burden men often feel trying to do good in many areas of their lives.[1] Christensen explains his painting:

> Did you ever feel the weight of the world on your shoulders? When I painted "The Burden of the Responsible Man" I felt overwhelmed by how much everybody expected from me. I felt as if life was taking everything I had and not giving much back, just dangling a carrot to keep me going. Even this man's pet, a hedgehog, needs to be fed and taken for walks, but is too prickly to offer warm "cuddlies" in return. But the man's a responsible person and so he just keeps plodding along. That's the point. I just kept plodding along, too, and things got better. I discovered that my burdens were really blessings and challenges necessary for my growth.[2]

I love how Christensen painted a hat full of people who are dangling a carrot. Who are they? A spouse? Children? Extended family? Friends? Coworkers? Who motivates us to keep going? Do we carry our heavy load for them? What people in our lives give our tasks meaning? We think frequently of significant people in our lives; we pray for them, we sacrifice for them, we work for them, and we will do whatever it takes to help them. They give us purpose. They give our mortal walk meaning. They give us motivation to waddle along, prickly hedgehog and all.

Christensen painted a companion piece called *The Responsible Woman*, in which he pays tribute to women's many roles and the daily loads they carry. He portrays a woman loaded with responsibility as a mother, homemaker, scheduler, baker, scholar, musician, gardener, sewer, pet owner, and decorator. She is beautifully dressed and flies through the air holding a candle of hope.[3]

This painting reminds me of the marvelous work women do every day. Yet many of them get discouraged as they try to do good and be good. They want to do God's will, but the endless number of good

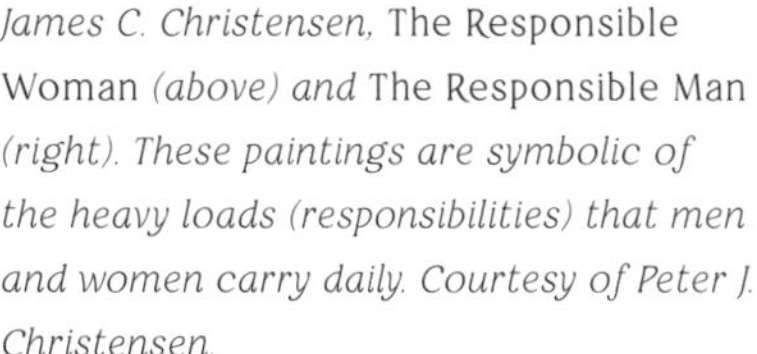

James C. Christensen, The Responsible Woman *(above) and* The Responsible Man *(right). These paintings are symbolic of the heavy loads (responsibilities) that men and women carry daily. Courtesy of Peter J. Christensen.*

things they might do is overwhelming. They get discouraged because they want to *do it all* but feel they inevitably fall short. I wonder if many women feel like I do sometimes—instead of flying from task to task, I often crawl, huffing and puffing and hoping my candle won't blow out!

As people genuinely trying to do good, we strive to keep our candles lit, held up high, with confidence that we are doing God's work. Then the wind of exhaustion blows our candles out. You may relate to these examples: Rachel studies for hours each day, works at the doughnut shop, cheers with her squad at games, and tries to spend time with her fiancé, and she breaks down crying because she can't do it all with a torn Achilles tendon. Michael works full-time, coaches his daughter's soccer team, serves as elders quorum president, and helps his aging parents, and he worries about not being a better father. Barbara juggles her time as Parent-Teacher Association (PTA) president, high school teacher, Sunday School instructor, and mother of six children, and she breaks out with shingles because of stress. It's hard to find a person who doesn't have a full plate—with many respectable and worthwhile tasks to accomplish. Exhaustion also dims the confidence of those struggling with mental illness and health challenges. They may have one or two things on their to-do list but can focus only on keeping hope alive, and they celebrate if they complete one task. We are all unique, but we all strive to succeed.

We are familiar with the words of King Benjamin: "And see that all these things are done in wisdom and order; for it is not requisite that a man should run faster than he has strength. And again, it is expedient that he should be diligent, that thereby he might win the prize; therefore, all things must be done in order" (Mosiah 4:27). What is the prize? We know that our long-term reward is eternal life. But is there a short-term prize? For me, the reward of diligence is peace—peace that I did my best, peace that I contributed to someone's happiness, peace that I'm becoming a better me, and peace that I'm not running faster than I have strength.

What gets in the way of us savoring peace and feeling hope about our day-to-day efforts? Are we trying to accomplish too many things at once? Do we expect to be perfect in all we do? Do we feel guilty for not doing more? "We all need to remember: men are that they might have joy—not guilt trips!" said President Russell M. Nelson.[4] Some of us aren't trying to be perfect in everything—we just seek to do good and be good—but the list of all the good things we can do seems to be endless! What can we do so we don't feel overwhelmed?

The Savior Speaks to Us

Years ago, my dear sister Karen, seven months pregnant and the mother of five young children, discovered that she had a fast-growing lymphoblastic lymphoma. Given a 20 percent chance of living, she started chemotherapy the next day, on Christmas Eve. Those were tender days for me. Karen was a beloved sister and a dear and influential friend. I wanted to do all I could to help her, and I received a strong impression that I needed to do so. I was going to graduate school, teaching at the missionary training center (MTC), and serving as Relief Society president. After several months of trying to balance work, school, and my sister's care, I was totally exhausted. But when my family asked if I needed help, my usual response was "Oh no, I'm fine. I can do it." I thought it would be selfish to focus on my needs when my sister's needs were so great. I wondered, "Why am I so burned out when I'm trying to do good?" I remembered that when I prayed, I received impressions like "Today you need to take a nap," "Today you need to spend more time studying for your class," or "Today you should ask your mother to help." I ignored those daily promptings and attended only to the one big impression to help my sister—whom I dearly wanted to help!

The Lord was trying to teach me how to balance my time and energy so I could accomplish what was most essential at the moment. Eventually I realized that the most important thing was to pursue the best interest of the "whole"—all of us together as one unified group: God, family, others, and myself. I learned to ask in prayer, "What is the most needful thing I can do today to help all of us together as *one*?" I had to seek inspiration about how to nurture all my relationships, including the one with myself—I was in the group of people to care for. In our attempt to serve God and others, taking care of ourselves is essential. We are part of the "whole," and sometimes the most important thing to do is take a nap!

That experience helping my sister taught me that the Lord will provide guidance about how best to use our time and energy. He helped me understand what was most needful and gave me peace that my efforts were sufficient in His eyes. I knew that for Him to help me manage my time, I needed to give *Him* time.

In commemoration of God the Father inviting the Prophet Joseph to "hear" His Son, Jesus Christ, President Nelson encouraged us to hear Him—to hear the voice of Christ. "That admonition given to Joseph is for each of us. We are to seek, in every way we can, to hear Jesus Christ, who speaks to us through the power and ministering of the Holy Ghost."[5] I feel Christ's direct interest in me when I read the

Doctrine and Covenants. I love how several sections begin with His invitation to hear Him: "Wherefore the voice of the Lord is unto the ends of the earth, that all that will hear may hear" (Doctrine and Covenants 1:11). "Listen to the voice of Jesus Christ, your Lord, your God, and your Redeemer" (Doctrine and Covenants 27:1).

We are promised in our baptismal and sacramental covenants that we will have the companionship of the Holy Ghost to always be with us. "President Lorenzo Snow declared that it is 'the grand privilege of every Latter-day Saint . . . to have the manifestations of the spirit every day of our lives.'"[6] We trust that God the Father, Jesus Christ, and the Holy Ghost work in harmony to minister to our needs. I will refer to this divine help from heaven as the voice of Christ.

Elder Neal A. Maxwell teaches us how to listen to the voice of Christ that helps us accomplish our daily tasks: "Life in the Church soon teaches us, too, that the Lord does not ask us about our ability, but only about our availability. And then, if we demonstrate our dependability, the Lord will increase our capability."[7] The Lord waits patiently for us to be *available* to listen to the still, small voice. Then we demonstrate our *dependability* by heeding the impressions we receive, and in turn He enhances our *capability*.

First, how can we make ourselves available to hear the voice of our Savior?

Be Available to Hear the Savior's Voice

In the thirteenth century, Catholic monks were instrumental in the invention of the clock.[8] They needed a way to carefully track time so they could remind one another when it was time to turn their thoughts heavenward—time to sing, time to pray, time to honor God, time to connect themselves to the divine power that gave them purpose and meaning. Initially the monks used candles with markings to indicate when they needed to rise and pray. Since they prayed and sang together every few hours, they would assign a monk to watch the candles. When the candles burned down to the next marking, the monk would wake the others. Later they turned to a bell system; someone would ring the bell when it was time to pray and sing. Again and again, the monks would join together to turn their thoughts to God. Eventually they invented a system with numbers in a circle on a round board so they could be even more precise—to the minute. It is the time-tracking instrument we know as a clock. The clock reminded the monks when they needed to turn their thoughts heavenward.

Today many of us have little clocks on our wrists. Our watches help us keep track of time—but time to do what? If you are like me, you carefully watch the time to see how much you can cram into one day. Amid all our daily tasks, are we taking time for the most essential actions that will turn our thoughts heavenward and allow us to call down the powers of heaven? Do we plan and prepare a specific time to hear Him?

We have many demands and responsibilities. We must choose to take time to be still and listen to the voice of Christ. We learn in Revelation 3:20 that Christ is waiting for us to invite Him into our lives: "Behold, I stand at the door, and knock: if any man hear my voice, and open the door, I will come in to him, and will sup with him, and he with me." Christ may be knocking, but we can't hear Him if we are distracted or if we have chosen to spend our time on other things.

What distracts us from being available to hear guidance from the Lord? One of our greatest distractions is technology—smartphones, television, radio, and the internet. Studies showed that in 2019 roughly three in ten Americans—and 48 percent of those ages eighteen to twenty-nine—were online "almost constantly."[9] Seven in ten Americans used social media, spending an average of two hours and three minutes on it each day.[10] American teens spent over seven hours a day on media—not including screen use for school or homework.[11] As for smartphones, Americans spend four to five hours a day just on their smartphones. One 2017 report stated that they "check their phones on average once every 12 minutes—burying their heads in their phones 80 times a day."[12]

The influence of media and technology is powerful—for good and evil. The internet makes information widely accessible and is an effective tool for sharing the message of Jesus Christ, connecting families, and sustaining friendships. But media can also be a disabling distraction from what matters most, as described by Alexander Solzhenitsyn, a Russian writer awarded the 1970 Nobel Prize in Literature: "We may witness shameless intrusion on the privacy of well-known people under the slogan 'everyone is entitled to know everything.' But this is a false slogan, characteristic of a false era: people also have the right not to know, and it is a much more valuable one. The right not to have their divine souls stuffed with gossip, nonsense, vain talk. A person who works and leads a meaningful life does not need this excessive burdening flow of information. . . . The press [and media have] become the greatest power[s] within the western countries."[13] Solzhenitsyn wrote this in 1978, over forty years ago—before the internet was created! We can see how powerful the influence of media and technology has become. Are our "divine souls stuffed" with information that is not meaningful? Does our use of media add to the quality of our lives or distract us from what is most uplifting and encouraging?

Elder Dieter F. Uchtdorf said, "We sometimes get distracted by so many things that seem more enticing. Printed material, wide-ranging media sources, electronic tools and gadgets—all helpful if used properly—can become hurtful diversions or heartless chambers of isolation."[14] Is our use of media creating more self-doubt? Does it cause feelings of inadequacy and loneliness? We face disconnection and isolation when using technology becomes a solitary activity. One thirteen-year-old reported, "'I would rather be on my phone in my room watching Netflix than spending time with my family. That's what I've been doing most of the summer. I've been on my phone more than I've been with actual people.' That's the way her generation is, she says. 'We didn't have a choice to know any life without iPads or iPhones. I think we like our phones more than we like actual people.'"[15] No wonder we are battling isolation and disconnection in society today.

I frequently ask myself if the quantity and the quality of my media usage is helping me connect with God and others or is disconnecting me from precious relationships. When we want to unwind after a busy day, it's easy to overload on TV shows and social media. We may be enticed to check the latest Facebook and Instagram feeds, see the latest news on national affairs, and watch just one more episode in a Netflix series. Media easily captivates our time and attention.

One of our greatest challenges to hearing the voice of heaven is the clutter in the mind that builds up with media and technology use. How do we clear out that clutter? Perhaps we can learn from organizing consultant Marie Kondo. She has a popular system for uncluttering homes and encourages people to keep only tangible items that bring joy to their lives. In a similar way, we can think about what clutters our minds and spend time only on that which brings us joy and connects us in meaningful relationships. Can we clean out the clutter that "stuffs our divine souls" with anything that is not edifying and worthwhile?

Our challenge is to identify anything that distracts and disconnects us from meaningful relationships, especially with the Lord. What occupies our time? What do we choose to do with our twenty-four hours each day? Do we look at our clocks and set aside time to turn our thoughts heavenward—time in praying, time in studying the scriptures, time in pondering, time in uncluttering our minds and being *still*?

Are we *available* to hear the Savior's voice? If not, we are on our own. For me, the thought of trying to juggle the important tasks of daily living without help from heaven fills me with self-doubt. I know I can't do it alone. But I can do it with the Savior's voice to help me.

During Christ's visit to the Nephites, He looked at the multitude and assessed their availability to hear His voice: "I perceive that ye are weak, that ye cannot understand all my words which I am commanded of the Father to speak unto you at this time. Therefore, go ye unto your homes, and ponder upon the things which I have said, and ask of the

Father, in my name, that ye may understand, and *prepare your minds for the morrow*, and I come unto you *again*" (3 Nephi 17:2–3). I'm grateful for the Savior's waiting on us to prepare our minds. He promises to come to us when we take the time to hear His voice and ponder His words. He will come again and again and again. He is patiently waiting for us to be willing and ready to hear Him.

Listen for One Prompting at a Time

Several years ago on July 24, I took my mother to a Pioneer Day program. We sat in the wheelchair section directly in front of the walkway, where we watched several attendees stroll back and forth waiting for the program to begin. My mother started waving her arm and vocalizing in her unique way, hoping I would understand what she was trying to communicate. A stroke had crippled her ability to clearly speak; she "spoke" often but not with sounds that were recognizable—not one word.

For twenty minutes she talked and waved her arm to try to communicate with me. As I sat next to her, I went through a long list of questions: "Are you talking about the decorations? Are you too cold? Too hot? Are you in pain? Are you uncomfortable? Would you like to say hello to those cute kids? Do you feel sick?" I simply could not understand her. After several minutes and many questions, I felt overwhelmed. Likewise, she was frustrated with me because I couldn't understand her.

I began seeking a little divine help, and two words came into my mind: *pop* and *popcorn*. I looked at her and asked, "Mom, would you like some pop and popcorn?" She stopped waving her arm and started laughing. She looked at me as if she wanted to say, "Finally! Yes, please! See, it was just one simple request!" It dawned on me that she was pointing to people walking by with popcorn, and she wanted me to get her some, so I hopped up and bought her the treat.

As we ate our popcorn, I received a clear impression: "The Spirit works with you the same way. When you stop and ask, the Lord will give you one or two ideas at a time. He will not overwhelm you; He will provide just one or two thoughts." That impression was significant for me. After those several minutes of me feeling flustered with trying to figure out how to help my mother, it came down to one idea. Likewise, that experience helped me see how the voice of the Lord will simplify and clarify how to use my time and energy. I needed to be still for a moment, ask for help, and recognize the one strongest impression that came into my mind. Then I needed to try my best to follow that prompting.

The "pop and popcorn" experience reminded me of the contrast between thoughts from the adversary and thoughts from the Holy Spirit. The adversary attempts to discourage us with a long list of to-dos to distract and disable our efforts. The Holy Spirit works with us differently by giving us one or two impressions at a time, not ten or twenty that would be overwhelming. The Spirit speaks truth to us about our current state—in a loving and motivating way—one prompting at a time. Often we focus too much on the past or the future, but the Spirit can give us what we need now. This is comforting and hopeful for me because I can't follow twenty thoughts at once, but I *can* follow one.

On the days when we feel like the *Responsible Woman* or the *Responsible Man* carrying a heavy load, we can stop to listen for divine whisperings regarding our most needful tasks for the day. I'm inspired by many great examples of prioritizing our time and energy: A mother puts her to-do list on hold while she helps a crying teenager. A student forgoes a fun activity with friends to study for an exam. A friend helps a sick neighbor with an errand in between picking up kids from school. A woman takes a nap instead of going to work, because her body is screaming for attention. There are many worthy options for spending our time. The key is to focus on what matters *most* at the moment.

We often find that when we try to accomplish numerous things at the same time, we become our own *adversary* instead of *advocate*—we work against ourselves instead of helping ourselves. For example, we set ourselves up for stress when we schedule too many things that are unrealistic for us to accomplish in one day. On the other hand, we become our own *advocate* when we give ourselves a reasonable amount of time to accomplish our tasks. We help ourselves out when we don't *run faster than we have strength* (see Mosiah 4:27).

Some people have circumstances that make it hard to trim down tasks on their lists. One single mother working full-time said, "I would simplify my life, but there is nothing I can cut out. I can't put my kids on the back burner. I can't quit my job, or we'll have to live in the homeless shelter. I don't want to quit my calling as a Primary teacher because it brings me joy. How do I not 'run faster than I have strength'?" Some things are definitely outside our control. But what can we do with that which is under our control? Can we trust that we will be empowered with the strength and wisdom to successfully manage our day as we heed the voice of Christ?

Our task is to "be still" and listen, one day at a time, one impression at a time—"Listen to him who is the advocate with the Father, who is pleading your cause before him" (Doctrine and Covenants 45:3). The voice of the Lord will tell us not only what to do but how much to do. President Henry B. Eyring taught:

> The Master can help those of us feeling overwhelmed by our circumstances. In the hardest trials, as long as you have the power to pray, you can ask a loving God: "Please let me serve, this day. It doesn't matter to me how few things I may be able to do. Just let me know what I *can* do. I will obey this day. I know that I can, with Thy help."[16]

Receiving divine guidance to manage our daily loads requires recognition of revelation meant just for us. As a new missionary in the MTC, I had a teacher who challenged us to increase our ability to recognize personal revelation. She asked us to pray every night for one week. After each prayer, we were to review in our minds each plea for help, ask ourselves, "What do I think God would say to me?" and then write down the impressions we received on a note card. I noticed that some answers were my own thoughts—my best guesses from my own understanding. I also noticed that some answers were "aha" moments when I had clear, precise thoughts or ideas. I starred those ideas and knew they were impressions from the Holy Spirit. My teacher's challenge helped me identify more precisely what receiving personal revelation felt like to me. The Lord helps us understand what revelation feels like in a way that we will understand, whatever way of praying and pondering that may be.

It helps me to clarify my thoughts and feelings by writing them down. When I end my morning prayer, I pause for a minute and ask, "What is the most important thing for me to do right now?" As I think, "What do I think Heavenly Father would say to me?" and take time to pause and be still, I receive one or two impressions. Writing down impressions in a journal often helps me discern how to spend my time and energy.

Sometimes we may feel that we haven't received an answer to our prayers. Or we may worry that the ideas that come into our minds are our own thoughts, our own best guesses about what we should do. I feel this way frequently, but I think God expects us to use the wisdom we have thus far. If we take action and God wants us to do something different, we can trust He will tell us. But the key is to ask Him! As we "[wait] patiently on the Lord" (Doctrine and Covenants 98:2), we can move forward and act on the impressions that come to our minds.

As we listen for one prompting at a time instead of several at a time, we will feel less overwhelmed and more confident that we can handle the tasks in front of us. Knowing that we have the Lord's guidance and blessing on what is most needful now is empowering.

Be *Dependable* to Follow His Promptings

Successfully managing our day with help from heaven begins with being available and continues with letting God know that He can depend on us to act on the guidance He gives us.

President Thomas S. Monson was an inspiring example of dependability. His legacy centered on listening to and following promptings to serve others. He shared, "The sweetest experience I know in life is to feel a prompting and act upon it and later find out that it was the fulfillment of someone's prayer, or someone's need. And I always want the Lord to know that if He needs an errand run, Tom Monson will run that errand for Him."[17] We see examples of how the Lord depended on him again and again—for fifty-four years—as he served as an Apostle and as a prophet. When he was asked how he had time to serve, he replied, "I am a very simple man. I just do what the Lord tells me to do."[18] President Monson's example and teachings have been life-changing for me. He has motivated me to let God know that He can depend on me—which is my daily quest.

My friend Allen was taught to be dependable by his mission president. His president counseled missionaries to get on their knees to pray and not get up until they understood their next errand from the Lord. After Allen received an answer, he was to get up and go do it. This counsel taught him not only to be available for the Lord but also to be dependable to run His next errand. Can the Lord count on us to run His errands—to be an instrument in His hands?

The Lord waits on us to follow through on promptings we receive. In Abraham 4:10–21 we read an account of the Creation that includes the phrase "And the Gods watched . . . until they [the things they had ordered] obeyed," a phrase repeated (with varying wording) each day of the Creation process. Similarly, God rejoices in our day's accomplishments and then waits and watches until we obey His promptings. Our obedience to His will refines our character, preparing us for the next day of growth and opportunity. President Eyring taught, "God's purpose in creation was to let us prove ourselves. The plan was explained to us in the spirit world before we were born. . . . We rejoiced to know the test would be one of faithful obedience even when it would not be easy: 'And we will prove them herewith, to see if they will do all things whatsoever the Lord their God shall command them' [Abraham 3:25]."[19]

My sister taught me an important lesson when she said, "If we want help, we need to take it as it comes. We can't expect more if we don't act on what we have already received." Brigham Young taught:

> "For precept must be upon precept, . . . line upon line, . . . here a little, and there a little" [Isaiah 28:10]. That is, He gives a little to His humble followers to-day, and if they improve upon it, to-morrow He will give them a little more, and the next day a little more. He does not add to that which they do not improve upon, but they are required to continually improve upon the knowledge they already possess, and thus obtain a store of wisdom.[20]

It takes time and courage to act on impressions we receive. Thirty years ago, I was scheduled to leave for Russia to manage a new language program. I went to the temple one day and received a strong impression that I had made a wrong decision: I shouldn't go to Russia and should move home instead. It was embarrassing to tell the program director that I had changed my mind. He tried to resolve my concerns until I said, "I'm sorry, but I feel like it's the wrong thing for me to do." After spending four months studying Russian and preparing the program, I wanted to go, but I could not ignore the strong impression I felt. I moved home to enjoy Christmas with my family, and three weeks later, my sister-in-law Amy introduced me to my future husband! I'm thankful Amy acted on the impression she received, and I'm grateful I followed my prompting to stay home!

Some promptings are life-changing; others are not. We may feel we need to move across town, not knowing why, but we act anyway and then realize the move was in the best interest of a child. We may be prompted to bring a meal to a friend and then find out she was sick or in need of encouragement. We share stories of finding lost items because someone followed an impression: a toy found under the couch, car keys under a pile of books, a passport in the suitcase pouch, and, of course, the orthodontic retainer found in the garbage dumpster (which happened to me twice!).

Acting on the impressions and promptings we receive is our signal to God that we are dependable. He can count on us. We take time to listen and to act. When we doubt we can successfully accomplish all we need to do, we can depend on the voice of Christ to help us focus on what is most needful. Can He depend on us?

Daily asking, daily listening, and daily following one impression at a time make us dependable for the Lord. Little by little—day by day—He increases our capability to manage our daily load.

The Lord Increases Our *Capability*

Managing our time with home, family, children, work, school, church, and our many other responsibilities can be overwhelming. Like the woman in the *Responsible Woman* painting, we fly from task to task trying to do good and be good, and we tune in to the voice of heaven that offers hope and direction. Our candles of hope keep us pressing forward, no matter the load, no matter the difficulty, because we know God hears our prayers.

When we doubt our ability to manage our roles and responsibilities, we can turn to the calming and peaceful voice of the Lord. We will not be overwhelmed with promptings of everything we could or should be doing better. The Holy Spirit will give us one or two impressions at a time, in a loving and motivating way. As we seek the Spirit, we will doubt less and do more of what is most important.

Sister Sharon Eubank, First Counselor in the Relief Society General Presidency, offered encouragement about our daily efforts: "'Wherefore, be not weary in well-doing, for ye are laying the foundation of a great work' [Doctrine and Covenants 64:33]. . . . As we seek the Lord's will and strive to do it, we are assured that every small effort is accepted. . . . Doing *better* doesn't always mean doing *more*. And if you do just one inspired thing each day, you are nevertheless the Lord's agent. . . . Try. Pray. Trust. You don't have to do it all."[21]

Photo of my husband walking the Camino—in stillness. Photo by author.

When we are available and dependable, we recognize the Savior's voice and we desire to obey His promptings. In return, He increases our *capability* to accomplish all that is needful. We trust that He can make more of us than we can make of ourselves. Elder Maxwell taught us that God is more concerned with our availability than with our capability because He knows our possibilities: "Your personal possibilities . . . are immense, if you will but trust the Lord to lead you from what you are to what you have the power to become."[22]

Focusing on the voice of the Lord helps us manage our time and energy wisely. Walking the Camino de Santiago in Spain was an opportunity for me to be quiet, ponder, and listen. I was reminded that God was there for me, and I was motivated to show God that I was there for Him—to hear Him! God's attention is personal. It is serene. It is always filled with love and strength. My husband, John, relished the time we had to be "still" on our journey. In one journal entry he wrote, "The encounter with one's worth happens in quiet places, places undisturbed by digital intrusions and the obligations of the world of contingency. It happens when one is available for the unstructured sounds, sights, touches, tastes and feel of nature and open to the unscripted stories of fellow travelers. It happens as we learn to read the book of the world, turning its pages with our feet, as Paracelsus noted. This is not speed reading: it is hovering without a watch and savoring without a calendar. It is the experience of the quiet Camino."

The Lord is always available for us. Can we be available for Him? We can always depend on Him. Can He depend on us?

I imagine the Savior calling out to us to join Him: "Listen for my voice! 'Learn of me, and listen to my words; walk in the meekness of my Spirit, and you shall have peace in me' [Doctrine and Covenants 19:23]. You are doing a great work! I'll guide you—one task at a time, one prompting at a time."

Invitation: Focus on being available to listen for and follow one prompting at a time.

Think-in-ink journal challenge: Write down one way you could be more "still" and better listen to the Savior's voice. For one week, ask in prayer each day, "What is the most needful thing for me to do today?" Write down the impressions that come to your mind, and make a plan that day to follow through with them.

Notes

1. James C. Christensen, *The Burden of the Responsible Man*, 1989, oil on canvas, 13 × 17″.
2. James C. Christensen, quoted in "The Burden of the Responsible Man," ARTUSA, https://artusa.com/product_details.php?id=3164.
3. James C. Christensen, *The Responsible Woman*, 1992, oil on canvas, 23 × 18.5″.
4. Russell M. Nelson, "Perfection Pending," *Ensign*, November 1995, 86.
5. Russell M. Nelson, "Opening Message," *Ensign*, May 2020, 7.
6. Lorenzo Snow, in Conference Report, April 1899, 52; quoted in Dallin H. Oaks, "Revelation" (Brigham Young University devotional, September 29, 1981), 1, speeches.byu.edu.
7. Neal A. Maxwell, in "Quotations," *Liahona*, December 1982.
8. See Stewart Brand, *The Clock of the Long Now: Time and Responsibility* (New York: Basic Books, 1999), 42.
9. Andrew Perrin and Sara Atske, "About Three-in-Ten U.S. Adults Say They Are 'Almost Constantly' Online," Pew Research Center, March 26, 2021, https://pewresearch.org/fact-tank/2019/07/25/americans-going-online-almost-constantly/.
10. J. Clement, "Daily Social Media Usage Worldwide 2012–2019," Statista, February 26, 2020, https://statista.com/statistics/433871/daily-social-media-usage-worldwide/.
11. See Kristen Rogers, "US Teens Use Screens More Than Seven Hours a Day on Average—and That's Not Including School Work," CNN, October 29, 2019, https://cnn.com/2019/10/29/health/common-sense-kids-media-use-report-wellness/index.html.
12. SWNS, "Americans Check Their Phones 80 Times a Day: Study," *New York Post*, November 8, 2017, https://nypost.com/2017/11/08/americans-check-their-phones-80-times-a-day-study/.
13. Alexander Solzhenitsyn, "The Exhausted West," *Harvard Magazine*, July–August 1978, 23.
14. Dieter F. Uchtdorf, "Of Things That Matter Most," *Ensign*, November 2010, 20.

15. Jean M. Twenge, *iGen: Why Today's Super-Connected Kids Are Growing Up Less Rebellious, More Tolerant, Less Happy—and Completely Unprepared for Adulthood* (New York: Atria Books, 2017), 13.
16. Henry B. Eyring, "This Day," *Ensign*, May 2007, 90–91.
17. *On the Lord's Errand: The Life of President Thomas S. Monson* (Provo, UT: Brigham Young University, 2008), film, 58:48–59:15, https://ChurchofJesusChrist.org/study/video/feature-films/2009-09-01-on-the-lords-errand-the-life-of-thomas-s-monson.
18. Quoted in Heidi S. Swinton, *To the Rescue: The Biography of Thomas S. Monson* (Salt Lake City: Deseret Book, 2010), 4.
19. Eyring, "This Day," 89–90.
20. Brigham Young, in *Journal of Discourses* (London: Latter-day Saints' Book Depot, 1855), 2:2.
21. Sharon Eubank, "That We May All Sit Down in Heaven Together" (address, Brigham Young University Women's Conference, Provo, UT, May 3, 2018), https://ChurchofJesusChrist.org/inspiration/to-women-doing-better-doesnt-mean-doing-more; italics added.
22. Neal A. Maxwell, "I Am But a Lad," *Tambuli*, February 1982, 32.

chapter six

FOCUS ON HIS FORGIVENESS

Feelings of self-doubt come when we feel we are not worth or worthy of God's help. Because of the Savior's atoning sacrifice, we can be forgiven for our sins and wrongdoing. We can focus on our ability to repent—to change—and accept His love and forgiveness.

One Christmas my husband gave our family a pottery-mending kit that replicated the Japanese art technique called *kintsugi.* Kintsugi begins with flawed, imperfect, broken pieces of pottery. An experienced kintsugi artist applies a natural resin to the broken seams that makes them stronger than the bonds of the original material. Then the artist covers the crooked lines and cracks with gold, silver, or platinum powder, resulting in a beautiful work of art. Ceramics repaired with the kintsugi technique are highly valued for their unique beauty.

In addition to the mending kit and a set of dishes, my husband gave us a beautiful kintsugi bowl to help us visualize a finished masterpiece. We began our project. We dropped a few pieces from the set of dishes and watched them break into pieces. Each of us picked a broken dish and carefully applied the resin to the crooked and cracked edges, sanded the seams, and sprinkled on the powdered gold. Even though our dishes weren't as beautiful as those made by skilled kintsugi artists, they were still a reminder of how something that is broken can be transformed by a master into something beautiful and valued.

As a family we discussed several lessons we could apply from that activity. Creating our kintsugi artwork reminded us that we are all imperfect, like a shattered dish, and we must decide if we will receive help from our Savior and Redeemer. We all have flaws. No one is exempt. Some may feel broken because of sin. Others may feel broken because of weaknesses or the behavior of others. Civil rights activist Bryan Stevenson wrote, "We are all broken by something. We have all hurt someone and have been hurt. We all share the condition of brokenness even if our brokenness is not equivalent. . . . Our brokenness is also the source of our common humanity, the basis for our shared search for comfort, meaning, and healing. Our shared vulnerability and imperfection nurtures and sustains our capacity for compassion."[1] We become more compassionate as we see that we all need a little mending. In our culture we have a mindset that we should be flawless, as if a life without imperfections is a sign of true beauty and strength. But none of us is

Kintsugi *bowls can symbolize flaws and weaknesses that can become beautiful in the refining process. Photo by author.*

without imperfections. We all could use some gold sprinkled on our weak seams. As with kintsugi, mending "brokenness" produces priceless pieces of *soul work.*

In a devotional for BYU Education Week, Elder Jeffrey R. Holland taught why religion is essential for mending and healing: "Our English word *religion* comes from the Latin word *religare*, meaning 'to tie' or, more literally, 'to re-tie.' In that root syllable of *ligare* you can hear the echo of a word such as *ligature*, which is what a doctor uses to sew us up if we have a wound. . . . Religion is that which unites what was separated or holds together that which might be torn apart—an obvious need for us, individually and collectively, given the trials and tribulations we all experience here in mortality."[2]

In our religion, we praise a Savior who ties and reties us to Him. We praise Him as our Master Surgeon who binds our wounds, our brokenness, our imperfections, and anything that separates us from Him and one another. Christ came to help us become "at-one" with Him, not to be left "al-one." We are not broken pieces of pottery left with no hope of mending.

In a world today that has more people leaving religion behind, people are forgoing the healing power of the Son of God. To believe that religion can heal souls is the very key to one's progression in mortality. To be religious means that we seek divine assistance to heal and mend what is broken or imperfect. Do we trust in our Savior's refining influence? Do we know we are worth healing?

"You Are Worth It!"

Self-doubt often comes when we feel we are not worth or worthy of God's help. We feel we are too broken, too flawed—that we have just made too many mistakes for the Savior to love us, help us, or forgive us. Satan fills our minds with guilt, shame, and the fear that God has given up on us, that He no longer loves us or cares about us. Satan would have us believe that our worth is insufficient for God's grace. Nothing could be further from the truth!

Are we too harsh on ourselves because we are not perfect yet? Do we think our *worth* is determined by how *good* we are right now? My nephew shared with me some of the thoughts he had when he was battling perfectionism:

- "I am either going to do [this task] *perfectly*, or I'm not going to do it at all—there is no use trying."
- "If I don't live my life perfectly, then I will not have the Spirit with me."
- "If I don't [do it] *perfectly*, then I'm not *worth* anything, and others will think I'm a failure, and I'll tell myself that I'm a failure."[3]

Our weaknesses do not define our worth; God has already defined it. An article of faith about our divine worth might read, "We believe we are children of heavenly parents, made in their image and with the potential to become like them because they *love* us." We have reason to believe that we are *worth* loving! I imagine our Heavenly Father saying, "Because of who you really are, my child, you are worth helping, worth inspiring, worth forgiving, and worth loving. You belong to me—making the glory and grandeur of your worth divine!" If we are ever tempted to say, "I'm not worth anything," could we remember how God sees us? "Remember the worth of souls is great in the sight of God" (Doctrine and Covenants 18:10). My nephew sees himself differently now: as someone with great worth in God's eyes. That knowledge has motivated him to give his best effort and enjoy the journey through life more—even with imperfections.

While serving as Primary General President, Joy D. Jones taught that there is a difference between worth and worthiness: "They are not the same. Spiritual *worth* means to value ourselves the way Heavenly Father values us, not as the world values us. Our worth was determined before we ever came to this earth. . . . On the other hand, *worthiness* is achieved through obedience. If we sin, we are less worthy, but we are never worth less! We continue to repent and strive to be like Jesus with our worth intact. . . . No matter what, we always have worth in the eyes of our Heavenly Father."[4]

Not too long ago, one of my students doubted his worth because of his sins. "I don't think I am worthy of God's love," he shared. "I've made too many mistakes and committed too many sins. I find it hard to believe that the Savior could take someone as broken as me and see someone worth helping." My heart went out to him. The most important lesson we learn from the Savior about His atoning sacrifice is that He loves us! He made it possible to overcome physical and spiritual death because we are worth it. With all He has done for us, He seems to say, "I did it all for you, because *you* are worth it to *me*! I paid the price for your sins so you can be worthy of returning back to my presence—worthy of eternal glory." The Savior believes in us! He knows what we can become with Him. "For it is I that taketh upon me the sins of the world; for it is I that hath created them; and it is I that granteth unto him that believeth unto the end a place . . . eternally at my right hand" (Mosiah 26:23–24).

President Jones continued, "If the love we feel for the Savior and what He did for us is greater than the energy we give to weaknesses, self-doubts, or bad habits, then He will help us overcome the things which cause suffering in our lives. He saves us from ourselves."[5] Because the Savior suffered for us, He rescues us from our suffering. We honor Him as we doubt our worth less and do more to be worthy.

Our Savior's Willingness to Forgive

In the Gospel of John we read the story of a woman taken in adultery. The scribes and Pharisees judged and condemned both her and her sin. Then Jesus came, stooped to the ground, and wrote in the sand as He upbraided her accusers: "He that is without sin among you, let him first cast a stone at her. . . . And they which heard it, being convicted by their own conscience, went out one by one." Jesus then approached the woman and said, "Woman, where are those thine accusers? hath no man condemned thee? She said, No man, Lord. And Jesus said unto her, Neither do I condemn thee: go, and sin no more" (John 8:3–11).

We learn two important lessons from the Savior's response. First, Jesus did not condemn the woman; He confirmed her divine worth, and He forgave her. Second, Jesus did not condone her sin. The woman needed to "sin no more"; she needed to repent. That is, she needed to grow. Repentance is growth under God's direction.

We can be at peace knowing that Christ came to save us from sin—not to condemn us as though we were ready for Final Judgment. We are not ready yet. Much growth is still needed. "For God sent not his Son into the world to condemn the world; but that the world through him might be saved. He that believeth on him is not condemned" (John 3:17–18). Christ came to save us from wrongdoing—we just need to believe Him!

Christ pleads our cause before the Father, even as He did for those who had put Him on the cross: "Father, forgive them [the soldiers]; for they know not what they do" (Luke 23:34). Christ was able to see beyond their horrific behavior, perceive their limited understanding, and know what possibilities of change were still theirs—even then, on the cross. Christ's response is a witness to all of us that He is willing to forgive. It's hard to fathom the depth of His compassion. If Jesus Christ is willing to forgive those who nailed Him to the cross, is He not also willing to forgive me and you for our sins? I believe He is willing. I stand in awe of His mercy. I love Him and will forever be grateful for what He has done for each one of us.

Sin takes a toll on our self-esteem. When we sin, we judge ourselves to be unworthy of the Perfect Judge's help. We hear people say, "I don't doubt that God can help me; I just doubt that I can stop my poor behavior, so I'm not worthy of God's help"; "I'm beyond help because of all the bad things I've done"; or "I have turned my back on God and assume He has turned His back on me." Author Brad Wilcox identifies these feelings as signs that we misunderstand the depth of the Atonement:

> We understand that God and Jesus were willing to forgive the first time, but we wonder how many more times they will be willing to watch us bumble along before they finally roll their eyes and declare, "Enough already!" We struggle so much to forgive ourselves that we wrongly assume God must be having the same struggle. . . .
>
> Christ Himself answers, "As often as my people repent will I forgive them their trespasses against me" (Mosiah 26:30; see also Moroni 6:8). Would Christ command us to "continue to minister" to the afflicted (3 Nephi 18:32) if He were not willing to continually minister to us in our afflictions?[6]

I love Brother Wilcox's statement that Christ will continue to minister to us—even when we have acted poorly, even when we have sinned. Why will He continue to minister to us? Because that is His work and His glory. He can see the end from the beginning and knows what we are capable of becoming.

Sometimes we confuse sin and weakness. Psychologist Wendy Ulrich explains that sin is willful rebellion against God, whereas weakness refers to human limitations and vulnerabilities. When we sin, repentance is needed to align our hearts and behavior with the will of God. But weaknesses are not sins. They are not rebellion against God; repentance is not needed. What is needed is humility.[7]

Some people feel guilty about having weaknesses, as if having weaknesses is a sin: "I feel so guilty for not being a better mother." "I'm ashamed that I'm not smarter." "I feel bad that I'm a terrible communicator." Did these people defy the will of God? If not, they have not committed sin. They may have weaknesses they need help with, but they have not rebelled against God—an important distinction.

Our Savior can forgive our sins and help us overcome our weaknesses. While there is always room for improvement, so many of us are doing better than we think we are. Can we stop feeling guilty for weaknesses that are not sins? Can we strive to have a humble heart and seek the Lord's help in overcoming both?

Humility requires submissiveness to the will of our Savior, which opens our hearts to personal refinement. In 1987 I participated in a BYU study abroad trip to Israel as a college student. One of the highlights of the trip was our visit to a potter's shop. We watched the potter work the clay on his potter's wheel. It was fascinating to watch him as he molded a pot, repeatedly adding more water and more clay. As he saw imperfections in his piece, he smoothed out the rough edges or started over with the mass of clay to make it bigger and better than before. The goal was to keep refining the piece until it was finished and complete. As a group we read Jeremiah 18:6: "Cannot I do with you as this potter? saith the Lord. Behold, as the clay is in the potter's hand, so are ye in mine hand."

That experience in Israel made a lasting impression on me. I pondered, "In what ways am I like clay in His hands? What does the Lord do with me if He is my potter?" Elder Neal A. Maxwell taught, "If faithful, we end up acknowledging that we are in the Lord's hands and should surrender to the Lord on His terms—not ours. . . . It is only by yielding to God that we can begin to realize His will for us. And if we truly trust God, why not yield to His loving omniscience? After all, He knows us and our possibilities *much better than do we*."[8] I learned that if I trust God, He can make more of me than I can. I needed to be spiritually submissive—submitting my will to God's will—which requires a humble heart.

Jesus Christ has promised to help us whenever we turn our hearts to Him and seek to receive His refining influence. Just as a kintsugi artist takes a broken pot and mends and beautifies fractured seams to create a work of art, Jesus Christ takes our sins, imperfections, and inadequacies and refines our character, improving us beyond our original state. We become more beautiful than we can imagine. The most essential part of this refining process is the Savior's forgiveness.

When we experience doubt about our worth or worthiness, can we remember the Savior's belief in our worth and His willingness to forgive our sins? Doctrine and Covenants 61:2 reminds us, "For I, the Lord, forgive sins, and am merciful unto those who confess their sins with humble hearts." The Savior asks us to be obedient so that we may be worthy of His blessings. President Ezra Taft Benson taught, "When obedience ceases to be an irritant and becomes our quest, in that moment God will endow us with power."[9] If our quest is to see how good we may become, we seek to be obedient. We seek to repent of our sins, knowing that the Savior is willing to forgive.

Repentance

For many of us, the word *repentance* is connected with feelings of guilt and shame and implies that we should feel bad about ourselves. Or perhaps we think repentance is necessary only for those who have committed *big* sins. But recently President Russell M. Nelson taught us:

> Does *everyone* need to repent? The answer is yes.
>
> Too many people consider repentance as punishment—something to be avoided except in the most serious circumstances. But this feeling of being penalized is engendered by Satan. He tries to block us from looking to Jesus Christ, who stands with open arms, hoping and willing to heal, forgive, cleanse, strengthen, purify, and sanctify us.

> The word for *repentance* in the Greek New Testament is *metanoeo*. The prefix *meta-* means "change." . . .
>
> Thus, when Jesus asks you and me to "repent," He is inviting us to change. . . .
>
> When we choose to repent, we choose to change! We allow the Savior to transform us into the best version of ourselves. . . . We choose to become more like Jesus Christ![10]

I have caught myself ignoring this concept of repentance, thinking it really didn't apply to me; I didn't have *big* sins, so I didn't need to think about repentance. But our prophet's invitation to choose *change* has been a powerful reminder that we are choosing to let our Savior "transform us into the best version of ourselves." And that is powerful motivation to choose repentance. One friend said that she applies a "growth mindset" (as explained in chapter 4) to repentance: "I see repentance as an opportunity for me to become better. It's how I can learn and grow and be a better me."

Our relationship with God changes when we realize that continually growing is what we were designed to do. This is the process by which we become more godlike, one day at a time. Repentance shouldn't be something we avoid but something we embrace. One sister shared her change of attitude about repentance:

> Formerly I had pictured God as a stern, finger-shaking personage who was impossible to please. I had been taught that he loved me, but since I didn't feel lovable I had built a barrier between us that made his love for me seem academic and meaningless. I was so overwhelmed by my distorted view of gospel "demands" and by my own lack of perfection that I could find little joy, comfort, or strength in the gospel—that which should have been my greatest resource.
>
> . . . [Then I realized that] God was my Friend. He had a smile on his face and had abundant approval and encouragement for me. I realized that he truly wanted me to experience the joy of learning and growing. . . .

> . . . Now I think of *repentance* as *growth*, and forsaking sin means avoiding things that limit growth. I now find myself free of the terrible burden of guilt, inadequacy, and fear of not "making it" that used to haunt me. Instead of feeling overwhelmed by my weaknesses, I feel a genuine desire to grow.[11]

Willingness to change produces growth. And growth and progress create joy. "For, behold, the Lord your Redeemer . . . suffered the pain of all men, that all men might repent and come unto him. . . . And how great is his joy in the soul that repenteth!" (Doctrine and Covenants 18:11–13). My favorite story about someone who had the courage to change and found joy in repenting is that of Alma the Younger. Alma was a rebel; he turned his back on God, committed many sins, and sought to destroy the Church of God. After an angel appeared to him, he had a mighty change of heart and became a great witness of Jesus Christ:

> And it came to pass that as I was thus racked with torment, while I was harrowed up by the memory of my many sins, behold I remembered also to have heard my father prophesy unto the people concerning the coming of one Jesus Christ, a Son of God, to atone for the sins of the world. . . .
>
> And oh, what joy, and what marvelous light I did behold; yea, my soul was filled with joy as exceeding as was my pain!
>
> Yea, I say unto you, my son, that there could be nothing so exquisite and so bitter as were my pains. Yea, and again I say unto you, my son, that on the other hand, there can be nothing so exquisite and sweet as was my joy. (Alma 36:17, 20–21)

We may have people close to us that are in need of an Alma-like experience. We desire that they may know of the joy made possible through our Savior. Turning away from God and relying on our own strength can be painful. But the amazing peace and joy Christ provides is ours if we choose to change. President Dallin H. Oaks taught, "The gospel of Jesus Christ challenges us to change. . . . The purpose of the gospel is to transform common creatures into celestial citizens, and that requires change."[12] When we think about our divine potential, it seems obvious that everyone needs to change—a lot—to get from where we are to where we need to be eventually. So why are we so afraid of change? Where can we start?

We can start by thinking about what God would have us change today. One of my friends suggested that we ask ourselves, "What is one thing I am *not* doing in my life that I should be doing?" or "What is one thing that I *am* doing right now that I should *not* be doing?" Remember, the adversary likes to overwhelm us with a long list of what we could be doing better, but the Holy Spirit does not work with us that way; He gives us one or two promptings at a time in a loving and motivating manner.

Change is achievable one step at a time. We can listen to the Spirit for guidance on the most important thing we can change right now. We can also ask the Lord in prayer, "What lack I yet?" Elder Larry R. Lawrence invited us to "humbly ask the Lord the following question: 'What is keeping me from progressing?' In other words: 'What lack I yet?' [After asking,] wait quietly for a response." He shared some examples of people who asked this question and what the Spirit whispered to them:

> A humble young man who couldn't seem to find the right young woman went to the Lord for help: "What is keeping me from being the right man?" he asked. This answer came into his mind and heart: "Clean up your language." . . .
>
> A single sister bravely asked the question: "What do I need to change?" and the Spirit whispered to her, "Don't interrupt people when they are talking." . . .
>
> . . . [A girl in college] fell to her knees and cried out, "What can I do to improve my life?" The Holy Ghost whispered, "Get up and clean your room." . . .
>
> . . . "It is our duty to be better today than we were yesterday, and better tomorrow than we are today" [Joseph Fielding Smith, *Doctrines of Salvation*, comp. Bruce R. McConkie, 3 vols. (1954–56), 2:18].[13]

Change can be big or small. We can change big bad habits, little bad habits, a sin, or a weakness. The process of change can begin with a simple prayer: "Please help me change _____." "Please forgive me for _____." I believe the Lord hears every plea for help to become a better person.

Our willingness to repent welcomes a better version of ourselves. We have an opportunity to repent every Sunday when we partake of the sacrament. Elder D. Todd Christofferson taught, "The bread and water represent the flesh and blood of Him who is the Bread of Life and the Living Water, poignantly reminding us of the price He paid to redeem us. . . . Figuratively eating His flesh and drinking His blood has a further meaning, and that is to *internalize the qualities and character of Christ* [His holiness], putting off the natural man and becoming Saints 'through the Atonement of Christ the Lord' [Mosiah 3:19]."[14] When we partake of the sacrament, we partake of the divine nature of Christ—of godliness. We become a little more godlike with each partaking. I have a friend who said, "Since I have an invitation each week to partake of godliness, I don't want one week to pass without me partaking of divinity to get me through the next week." Her statement has reminded me personally of the power of this sacred ordinance. Christ's gift to us on a weekly basis is to partake of His power, His love, and His strength as we symbolically *internalize* His atoning sacrifice for us.

The beauty of the Atonement is that Christ already paid the price for us to progress. Now it's up to us to accept His help. He is our Savior and our Friend: He paid the price for us to be forgiven from sin, and His encouragement is constant. In the hymn "Reverently and Meekly Now," we sing:

> In the solemn faith of prayer
> Cast upon me all thy care,
> And my Spirit's grace shall be
> Like a fountain unto thee.

At the throne I intercede;
For *thee* ever do I plead.
I have loved thee as thy friend,
With a love that cannot end.

Be obedient, I implore,
Prayerful, watchful evermore,
And be constant unto me,
That thy Savior I may be.[15]

When we choose to repent, we invite the Savior to go to work on us. Our willingness to change calls down the redeeming power of the Savior that molds and refines us into something more beautiful, like an artist's masterpiece.

Our Forgiveness—Emulating the Atonement

During one class period at BYU, I shared a quote from President Boyd K. Packer with my students: "The Lord provides ways to pay our debts to him. In one sense, we ourselves may participate in an atonement. When we are willing to restore to others that which we have not taken, or heal wounds that we did not inflict, or pay a debt that we did not incur, we are emulating His part in the Atonement."[16] I then asked my students, "How can we emulate the Atonement?" One student said, "I can wash dishes that I did not dirty and clean up messes that I did not make." Another said, "I can forgive someone who made no apology." And another, "When my roommate drives me crazy, I can be patient anyway."

My husband, John, taught at a BYU Women's Conference, "While we do not have the power to blot out our spouse's sins or offenses, we can heal each other when we imitate the merciful dimension of the Savior's memory—His kind forgetfulness."[17] We don't have the redemptive power unique to the Savior, but we can imitate His loving-kindness and His forgiveness. When someone acts poorly, we can love that person anyway, be patient anyway, serve him or her anyway, and be a good example anyway. Can we look beyond poor behavior and focus on the person's potential? Can we not be easily offended and instead look for the need behind an irritating behavior? Let us try to fill in the gaps where someone is weak, comfort those that stand in need of comfort, and mourn with those that mourn (see Mosiah 18:9). We help others and ourselves when we extend the Savior's loving-kindness and forgiveness.

The Savior offers hope in His forgiveness and wants us to experience the peace that accompanies it. He also requires that we forgive others and seek to be instruments in His hands: "For if ye forgive men their trespasses, your heavenly Father will also forgive you" (Matthew 6:14).

Elder Timothy J. Dyches retold how Corrie ten Boom, a Holocaust survivor, was able to receive and then extend the Savior's love and forgiveness:

> Corrie ten Boom, a devout Dutch Christian woman, found . . . healing despite having been interned in concentration camps during World War II. She suffered greatly. . . .
>
> After the war she often spoke publicly of her experiences and of healing and forgiveness. On one occasion a former Nazi guard who had been part of Corrie's own grievous confinement in Ravensbrück, Germany, approached her, rejoicing at her message of Christ's forgiveness and love.
>
> "'How grateful I am for your message, *Fraulein*,' he said. 'To think that, as you say, He has washed my sins away!'
>
> "His hand was thrust out to shake mine," Corrie recalled. "And I, who had preached so often . . . the need to forgive, kept my hand at my side.
>
> "Even as the angry, vengeful thoughts boiled through me, I saw the sin of them. . . . Lord Jesus, I prayed, forgive me and help me to forgive him.

> "I tried to smile, [and] I struggled to raise my hand. I could not. I felt nothing, not the slightest spark of warmth or charity. And so again I breathed a silent prayer. *Jesus, I cannot forgive him. Give me Your forgiveness.*
>
> "As I took his hand the most incredible thing happened. From my shoulder along my arm and through my hand a current seemed to pass from me to him, while into my heart sprang a love for this stranger that almost overwhelmed me.
>
> "And so I discovered that it is not on our forgiveness any more than on our goodness that the world's healing hinges, but on His. When He tells us to love our enemies, He gives, along with the command, the love itself."[18]

Corrie ten Boom learned a life-changing lesson: the Nazi guard was also worthy of the Savior's love and forgiveness—even after all the horrible things he had done. His deeds were unworthy, but his soul was worth redeeming. She was able to feel the Savior's love work through her because she was willing to forgive. (There are additional principles that must be addressed with the complexity of circumstances regarding abuse. Only basic principles are addressed here.)

Peter asked Jesus, "How oft shall my brother sin against me, and I forgive him? till seven times? Jesus saith unto him, I say not unto thee, Until seven times: but, Until seventy times seven" (Matthew 18:21–22). God asks that we always forgive, and He promises that something beautiful will happen to our hearts when we do: we will feel the Savior's goodness and grace and want to share it with others.

Forgiveness is essential for overcoming self-doubt. President James E. Faust taught:

> If we can find forgiveness in our hearts for those who have caused us hurt and injury, we will rise to a higher level of self-esteem and well-being. Some recent studies show that people who are taught to forgive become "less angry, more hopeful, less depressed, less anxious and less stressed," which leads to greater physical well-being

> [Fred Luskin, in Carrie A. Moore, "Learning to Forgive," *Deseret Morning News*, Oct. 7, 2006, p. E1]. Another of these studies concludes "that forgiveness . . . is a liberating gift [that] people can give to themselves" [Jay Evensen, "Forgiveness Is Powerful but Complex," *Deseret Morning News*, Feb. 4, 2007, p. G1].[19]

Forgiveness is a gift from God, a gift we can generously give to others—and to *ourselves*. Sometimes we forget that we need to forgive ourselves too. In a BYU devotional, Steven M. Sandberg, assistant to the president of BYU, taught:

> You are worth being and feeling forgiven; and . . . our Savior wants to help you forgive yourself. . . .
>
> When you find that your inner critical voice is louder than your compassionate voice [toward yourself], imagine what you might say to a close friend in a similar situation. You would sit with them in empathy. You would offer words of hope. You would point out their strengths and remind them that they are loved. I know Christ would do this for you if He sat beside you.
>
> Can you become that friend to yourself? When Christ asks us to act with compassion unto "the least of these," that includes you and how you treat yourself [Matthew 25:40].[20]

Again, sometimes *you* are the person you most need to forgive!

As we participate in the repentance process, we are reminded that God believes in us more than we believe in ourselves. He loves us more than we love ourselves because we belong to Him; we are His family, and He knows what we can become.

Putting Our Trust in the Hands of God

A few years ago, our family went to the Accademia Gallery Museum in Florence, Italy, where we saw many of Michelangelo's masterpieces. I'll never forget seeing the statue of *David* for the first time and wondering

Michelangelo (1475–1564), Atlas Slave. *One of Michelangelo's* Prisoners *statues that are still in the process of becoming perfected—just like us. Courtesy of Jörg Bittner Unna. Wikipedia.org.*

how someone could create something so perfect. We saw many impressive pieces of marble that portrayed the majesty of the human body. The ones I found most intriguing were the statues that were only partially carved; they looked as if the figures were trying to break out of the stone. You could see only part of a finished masterpiece, a beautiful person emerging from the rugged and unfinished edges. When Michelangelo was asked how he created a magnificent statue of an angel, he reportedly replied, "I saw the angel in the marble and carved until I set him free."[21]

Perhaps one of the reasons Michelangelo left these pieces unfinished—*non finito*—was to illustrate, like kintsugi artists, the beauty of imperfection. His figures, like each of us, struggle to free themselves from whatever binds them. Scholars claim that Michelangelo deliberately left these statues (called the *Prisoners*) incomplete to represent the "struggle of man to free the spirit from matter."[22] The problem many feel is that we are prisoners stuck in a state of weakness that prevents us from seeing our potential as masterpieces. We want to be free of the sins and weaknesses that constrain us.

We are like art, continually being refined by the hand of our Creator. He is our Master Sculptor, the Master of peace, creating a *masterpiece* in each one of us. With our limited vision, we may see only the rugged, jagged, unfinished edges that need refining. If we could see as God sees, we would perceive our *non finito* ("unfinished") magnificence simply because we are made in His image. We are His children with the potential to become like Him. He carves, molds, and refines us until we are perfected as He is—if we accept His help. We pray, "O Lord, thou art our father; we are the clay, and thou our potter; and we all are the work of thy hand" (Isaiah 64:8).

God knows us and our possibilities better than we do. Can we put our lives in His hands and accept His refining influence? Can we believe we are worth helping? Our Savior seeks to bless us. Can we seek to be worthy of His blessings?

The yellow arrow signs along the Camino point the way, which is like our need to receive directions to the right path in life. Photo by Allen Kreutzkamp.

On the Camino de Santiago, pilgrims frequently see yellow arrow signs that mark the path. These yellow arrows are painted on barns, buildings, poles, trees, rocks—you name it. The yellow arrows ensure that pilgrims won't get lost. When sin causes us to get off the path as we walk our journey through life, repentance puts us back on the "Camino"—like yellow arrows pointing the way to becoming a better version of ourselves. Elder Dale G. Renlund taught that the Swedish word for repentance, *omvänd*, means "to turn around."[23] In the words of C. S. Lewis, repenting is "being put back on the right road."[24] The very process of repentance is about turning our hearts back to God. As we repent, God not only forgives us but confirms our worthiness to receive His blessings.

If we get off the path, Christ points the way back: "I am the *way*, the truth, and the life: no man cometh unto the Father, but by me" (John 14:6; italics added). I imagine Him reminding us, "I made the pathway back home possible for you. Repent and come unto me. Accept my refining influence because you are a child of God with divine potential—that makes you worth helping!"

Invitation: Focus on the Savior's desire and willingness to forgive you. Focus on how you can change, repent, and partake of the Savior's refining influence.

Think-in-ink journal challenge: Write down why you are thankful for the Savior's willingness to forgive. Identify and write down one thing you can change and work on right now (that is, one thing you are doing that you need to stop doing or one thing you are not doing that you should be doing).

Notes

1. Bryan Stevenson, *Just Mercy: A Story of Justice and Redemption* (New York: Spiegel and Grau, 2015), 289.
2. Jeffrey R. Holland, "Religion: Bound by Loving Ties" (Brigham Young University Education Week address, August 16, 2016), 1, speeches.byu.edu.
3. Devin Vogelsberg, email message to author, May 28, 2020.
4. Joy D. Jones, "Value beyond Measure," *Ensign*, November 2017, 14.
5. Jones, "Value beyond Measure," 15.
6. Brad Wilcox, *The Continuous Atonement* (Salt Lake City: Deseret Book, 2009), 14–15.
7. See Wendy Ulrich, *Weakness Is Not Sin: The Liberating Distinction That Awakens Our Strengths* (Salt Lake City: Deseret Book, 2009), 21–37.
8. Neal A. Maxwell, "Willing to Submit," *Ensign*, May 1985, 72; italics added.
9. Quoted by Donald L. Staheli, "Obedience—Life's Great Challenge," *Ensign*, May 1998, 82.
10. Russell M. Nelson, "We Can Do Better and Be Better," *Ensign*, May 2019, 67.
11. Louise Brown, "Learning to Love Myself," *Ensign*, March 1982, 30.
12. Dallin H. Oaks, "Repentance and Change," *Ensign*, November 2003, 37.
13. Larry R. Lawrence, "What Lack I Yet?," *Ensign*, November 2015, 33–35.
14. D. Todd Christofferson, "The Living Bread Which Came Down from Heaven," *Ensign*, November 2017, 37; italics added.
15. "Reverently and Meekly Now," *Hymns*, no. 185; italics added.
16. Boyd K. Packer, "The Brilliant Morning of Forgiveness," *Ensign*, November 1995, 20.
17. John R. Rosenberg, "'Old Variaunce' or 'Newe Attonement': Marriage and the Imitation of Christ," in *A Light Shall Break Forth: Talks from the 2005 BYU Women's Conference* (Salt Lake City: Deseret Book, 2005), 192–93.
18. Timothy J. Dyches, "Wilt Thou Be Made Whole?," *Ensign*, November 2013, 38–39.
19. James E. Faust, "The Healing Power of Forgiveness," *Ensign*, May 2007, 68.
20. Steven M. Sandberg, "The Light of Forgiving" (Brigham Young University devotional, March 10, 2020), 5, speeches.byu.edu.

21. Quoted in David S. Baxter, "Overcoming Feelings of Inadequacy," *Ensign*, August 2007, 14.
22. "Michelangelo's Prisoners or Slaves," Accademia.org, http://www.accademia.org/explore-museum/artworks/michelangelos-prisoners-slaves/.
23. Dale G. Renlund, "Repentance: A Joyful Choice," *Ensign*, November 2016, 122.
24. C. S. Lewis, *The Great Divorce* (1946), 6; quoted in Renlund, "Repentance: A Joyful Choice," 122.

conclusion

FOCUS ON HIS INVITATION

Feelings of self-doubt may come when we rely on our own strength. The Savior offers to help us on our journey through mortality. He invites us to walk with Him and rely on His love, power, and strength. We can stay focused on Christ—the Light of the World and our Savior from self-doubt.

During our study abroad trip to Israel, our group visited historic places where the Savior walked and where many significant events occurred. One day we toured Hezekiah's Tunnel, which was built in about 701 BC to provide Jerusalem with a reliable source of water in the event of attack by the Assyrians. The tunnel extends more than 1,700 feet in length and is built in a zigzag pattern. Constructed in limestone rock, the tunnel brought the waters of the Gihon Spring outside the walls of Jerusalem to the pool of Siloam.[1]

The director of our program, Jeff, prepared us to walk through the tunnel by telling us to bring a flashlight and wear sturdy shoes. He warned us that the path would be rocky and that we might be walking in several inches of water. The first half of our walk through the tunnel was a fun adventure. The second half was a difficult challenge: Jeff asked us to turn off our flashlights and walk in the dark. I was stunned. Was he serious? How could I walk through the wet, rocky tunnel without light?

My heart began to race; I was scared to death, sure that I would fall on the rocks and land headfirst in the water that reached my knees. Most of all, I was nervous that I would panic from claustrophobia. However, I didn't want to be the only coward in our group, so I turned off my flashlight. Everything around me was pitch black. To make matters worse, I was the last person in line and worried that I would be left behind. As I tried to navigate the tunnel in the dark, my hands moving along the wet, slippery walls, I pleaded for help. I couldn't decide if I was frightened or just mad at Jeff for planning such a scary trip. All I knew was that I needed a little comfort.

At that moment, someone in another group about thirty feet behind me flashed a light for a split second, just long enough for me to see which way the tunnel was turning. The light assured me that I was OK. I continued walking forward in the dark, breathing deeply and trying to listen to the people in front of me. I noticed that just when I would become fearful again, I would see another flash of light, which would fill me once more with confidence and assurance. This happened six or seven times. I made it to the end of the tunnel in the dark with those occasional flashes of light. Often the light came when I was the most fearful and uncertain.

After reaching the end of the tunnel, our group cheered, laughed, and celebrated our accomplishment. I was relieved just to have survived the experience! I was thankful for the stranger behind me who gave me occasional light.

Walking through Hezekiah's Tunnel shows the need for light—like the divine light we need as we press forward on rocky paths. Photo by Sarah Bodine.

My whole life has been like that walk through Hezekiah's Tunnel. I have been deeply moved as I've pondered the times when I felt I had been walking in the dark and the Lord provided me light so I could see the way. When I've stumbled along the path, I've pleaded for help, and the Lord has given me flashes of inspiration to renew my hope and rekindle my faith. I've learned that if I keep going, keep believing, He will always show me the next step to take, a corner to turn, or a new path to follow. His divine light will keep me steady and secure on a somewhat rocky path.

I love the hymn "Lead, Kindly Light" by John Henry Newman: "The night is dark, and I am far from home; / Lead thou me on! / Keep thou my feet; I do not ask to see / The distant scene—one step enough for me."[2] I'm thankful for the Savior's light that allows me to walk "one step" more, the next step that is "enough"—enough to love my husband, to nurture my daughters, to help friends and family, to contribute at work. I can take one step at a time; that is enough.

Jesus taught us, "I am come a light into the world, that whosoever believeth on me should not abide in darkness" (John 12:46). Our belief in and dependence on His light will help us take the next step out of darkness into the light.

Walking Alone

Even with our knowledge of God's plan, we may still catch ourselves trying to walk our mortal journey without Him. Elder Robert D. Hales declared that we "can't do it alone," regardless of our level of spiritual maturity:

> We may know that God lives. We may know that Jesus is the Christ. We may know that he gave his life for our redemption, that he is resurrected that we might live, and that he is alive today. We may know that Joseph Smith has restored The Church of Jesus Christ of Latter-day Saints in the last dispensation of the fulness of times . . . a time when the scriptures that have been revealed to us are virtually all the scriptures available to mankind. . . . Yet, my brothers and sisters, with all of this knowledge, why is it that some of us fail to learn the very critical point that we did not come to this life to live it alone?[3]

A major obstacle to overcoming self-doubt is thinking or acting like we have to do it alone. With this belief, our path turns dark and discouraging. We end up feeling isolated from the strength we so desperately need. Many feel they don't need others to progress. Psychologist Brené Brown says, "One of the greatest barriers to connection is the cultural importance we place on 'going it alone.' Somehow we've come to equate success with not needing anyone. Many of us are willing to extend a helping hand, but we're very reluctant to reach out for help when we need it ourselves. It's as if we've divided the world into 'those who offer help' and 'those who need help.' The truth is that we are both.

. . . The heart of spirituality is connection. When we believe in that inextricable connection, we don't feel alone."[4]

Connection implies "I need you" and "You need me." Why is it destructive to walk our mortal journey alone? Because progression is relational. We need each other because our progress builds on relationships—with God, family, others, and ourselves. We help each other. We learn from each other. We love and care for each other. We learn how to put gospel principles into action with each other. We share how we navigate the ups and downs in our journey. We make covenants together that connect us to each other for the eternities.

Again, progression is relational. We need each other. There is so much goodness, talent, and strength around us to learn from. Each of us works hard to gain *independent* strength emotionally, mentally, socially, intellectually, physically, and spiritually. Then we become *interdependent*—everyone sharing the strength they've gained with each other. We become encircled with love and security—reminding us that we are not alone.

Sometimes we are unaware of the distracting influence of the adversary. Where Christ seeks to *enable* our progression, the devil seeks to *disable* our efforts. The word *disable* means to "put out of action[, to] prevent or discourage (someone) from doing something."[5] Satan's disabling influence blocks our view of the light of Christ. He seeks to handicap our happiness, paralyze our progress, and cripple our relationship with Christ. Satan knows that relationships are critical to our progress, and he seeks to do all he can to separate us from those who mean the most to us. He doesn't want us listening to or learning from God, and he doesn't want us listening to and learning from each other.

The Savior connects us. He does not want us to be alone! But Satan disconnects us. He triumphs when we are isolated, lonely, and separated from heaven's help.

Parents feel the heartache of children who choose to walk alone, without the help of God and others. One couple I know summarized an experience with their child this way:

> Our son no longer believes in God. He sees no need for religion or spirituality in his life. He thinks that—if by chance—God really does exist, God would not be interested in him. He stopped praying personally and with his family. He believes he will be "just fine on his own." He has cut off all connection to God and the Church. He talks a lot about being lonely. He feels bad that he doesn't have more friends but doesn't know where to find them. He suffers with low self-esteem and has little confidence in his ability to be successful. He is consumed with doubt about himself and his possibilities. *If only* he realized that the relationships he has severed are relationships that can help him to be happy and successful!

Our hearts break when we have family members who disconnect from God and the Church, because we know they are missing out on crucial experiences, such as the following:

- relationships with ward members who could offer love and support
- social activities at church that would provide the opportunity to meet new people and feel encouragement from others who are the same age
- testimony meetings and lessons at church that would inspire them
- family prayer, family scripture study, and home evening lessons that would help them feel connected to family
- personal prayer and scripture study that would remind them that God loves them

It is painful to see someone you love separate him- or herself from the relationships that channel divine help, family help, friend help, and church help. Elder Robert D. Hales explains why we need to walk our journey with God and others:

> The "isolated self" shut off from the Light of Christ makes us become fallible—open to delusion. The balance and perspective which come from caring about others and allowing others to care for us form the essence of life itself. We need the inspired help of others to avoid deceiving ourselves. It has always been a mystery to me why the intellectual elite sometimes shut themselves off from the Spirit of God. . . .
>
> It is also God's plan that we cannot return to his presence alone, without the help of someone else. . . .
>
> When you attempt to live life's experiences alone, you are not being true to yourself, nor to your basic mission in life. Individuals in difficulty often say: "I'll do it alone," "Leave me alone," "I don't need you," "I can take care of myself.". . .
>
> . . . I have also found in life that there is none too great to need the help of others. There is none so great that he can "do it alone."[6]

When we try to "do it alone," we focus on ourselves—on our own strength and our own wisdom. No wonder we feel consumed with self-doubt when we try to walk alone. No wonder we become impatient with ourselves, fret about our inadequacies, and feel overwhelmed with the tasks of life. Jesus Christ has a different message: we have help! Our Savior implores us, "Fear thou not; for I am with thee: be not dismayed; for I am thy God: I will strengthen thee; yea, I will help thee; yea, I will uphold thee with the right hand of my righteousness" (Isaiah 41:10).

The good news of the Atonement is that we are not isolated—we are not alone! We are not disconnected from help in our doubt and insecurity. We can be connected to the patient powers of heaven that can reach down and gather us together in love and strength. Christ prays in our behalf to be "at-one" with Him: "And now Father, I pray unto thee . . . that they may believe in me, that I may be in them as thou, Father, art in me, that we may be one" (3 Nephi 19:23). Christ invites us into perfect unity with Him and our Father. Do we accept His offer?

Christ's Gift Allows Us to Become One with Him

In Spain's Prado Museum hangs a large painting by Venetian artist Jacopo Tintoretto.[7] The painting portrays the moment before the Last Supper when the Savior washes the feet of the disciples. Anciently, a servant washed the feet of all guests who visited a home. Tintoretto depicts the Savior inviting His Apostles into a rented room and enacting the role of servant. The Apostles know that Jesus is the Son of God, and they are unsettled by His humble gesture. Tintoretto captures the moment in history when Jesus washed the feet of Peter, as recorded in the book of John: "Then cometh he to Simon Peter: and Peter saith unto him, Lord, dost thou wash my feet? Jesus answered and said unto him, What I do thou knowest not now; but thou shalt know hereafter. Peter saith unto him, Thou shalt never wash my feet" (13:6–8).

I will never forget the first time I saw Tintoretto's interpretation of Peter accepting Christ's service to him. The details of this painting that impressed me are the emotion in Peter's face, his outstretched arms, and his eyes riveted on the Savior. You can see the very moment when Peter understands the Savior when He declares, "If I wash thee not, thou hast

Tintoretto's painting of the Last Supper shows Peter accepting Christ's gift. Courtesy of the Prado Museum, Madrid, Spain.

no part with me" (John 13:8). This is the moment in Tintoretto's imagination when Peter understands that if he does not permit the Savior to serve him, then he cannot become "one" with Him. In order to emphasize the connection between washing and the Atonement, Tintoretto painted an inset image of the Last Supper directly above the Lord's head. Peter must have thought that he should be the one washing feet, not the Savior. However, at this moment, Peter understood that receiving Christ's service was symbolic of him receiving the Savior's gift of the Atonement. Hence, Peter's plea: "Not my feet only, but also my hands and my head" (John 13:9).

Do we hesitate, like Peter, to partake of Christ's gift to us, not understanding the nature of the service He extends to us, not feeling worthy of His offering, or not acknowledging the need to partake of His gift of service? In Doctrine and Covenants 88:33 we read, "For what doth it profit a man if a gift is bestowed upon him, and he receive not the gift? Behold, he rejoices not in that which is given unto him, neither rejoices in him who is the giver of the gift." Do we rejoice in the giver and the gift?

To become one with the Savior, and with others, we must receive His infinite service we call "atonement." To be "one" is another way of saying "complete, whole, and fully developed"—that is, perfect. Christ's greatest manifestation of love is His gift that allows us to become whole and complete as He is. We can't be "fully developed" by ourselves. The blessings of eternal life require being "complete"—unified in marriage and family relationships. Our divine refinement is not a solitary process but one that requires interaction and connection with others and with God.

The Atonement makes unity possible. "The life of Adam and Eve is the story of receiving the Atonement," explained Elder Bruce C. Hafen, "which empowered them to overcome their separation from God and all opposition until they were eternally 'at one,' with the Lord, and with each other."[8] Isn't this our story as well? Our story of receiving the Atonement? We accept Christ's gift to become "at-one" with Him, which enables us to become perfect as He is. Are we willing to accept His service, His gift, His help? Are we willing to allow the Savior to wash *our* feet? Are we willing to walk with *Him*?

Accepting Help from Jesus Christ

When I arrived in Spain to walk the Camino with my husband, I wanted to do something to honor Christ. How could I give Him a tribute that didn't feel trite? Nothing seemed like it would be good enough to honor Him who has given me everything! So I changed my question: "What has helped me the most to feel close to Him?" Reading the Book of Mormon was my first answer. I decided that I could honor Him by doing something powerful that drew me close to Him. Since I couldn't read as I walked, I listened to the audio version of the Book of Mormon. Hour after hour, as we walked through beautiful forests and quaint towns, I heard the words of Christ. It was a different experience going through this sacred book that fast instead of carefully reading just portions at a time. I could see the big picture of the entire book more clearly—the book's witness that the Savior and Redeemer of the world has come to help us. I heard repeated themes about trusting the Lord. I heard repeated warnings to beware of pride and to be humble and repent. I heard many stories with the same story line relating the consequences of people remembering God and forgetting God. Mostly, I heard an invitation to accept the Savior. My experience was sweet. My testimony was strengthened as I tried to honor Christ as I walked. Thankfully, He also walked with me.

"And now, remember the words of him who is the life and light of the world, your Redeemer, your Lord and your God" (Doctrine and Covenants 10:70). Precious are the words of the Book of Mormon that teach us about our relationship with Christ. The blessings of the Atonement remind us that we are not alone; we are invited into a unified relationship with Christ and our Father.

When we encounter self-doubt, when we feel we are not as good as we should be, we can remember that those feelings can help us recognize that we need help—first and foremost from the Savior. Sister Michelle D. Craig, First Counselor in the Young Women General Presidency, said, "The surprising truth is that our weaknesses can be a blessing when they humble us and turn us to Christ. Discontent becomes divine when we humbly approach Jesus Christ with our want, rather than hold back in self-pity. In fact, Jesus's miracles often begin with a recognition of want, need, failure, or inadequacy."[9]

Why do we need the Savior by our side when we doubt ourselves? Because He reminds us we can't do it on our own—we can't achieve the kind of progress required to become refined like He is. Because feeling His encouragement personally motivates us to keep trying. Because He reminds us that our mortal journey is about recognizing God's love and learning to love the way He does. Because He helps us focus less on our weaknesses and more on loving others. And because He reminds us that His love and strength are the very means by which we can become like Him—even while in our state of inexperience, imperfection, and weakness.

We can't experience the refining process of perfection without Christ. He molds and refines us into the glorious beings we are capable of becoming. And He is the only one who can do so. Sheri L. Dew taught:

> The Savior isn't our last chance; He is our only chance. Our only chance to overcome self-doubt and catch a vision of who we may become. . . .
>
> The Lord knows the way because He *is* the way and is our only chance for successfully negotiating mortality. His Atonement makes available all of the power, peace, light, and strength that we need to deal with life's challenges—those ranging from our own mistakes and sins to trials over which we have no control but we still feel pain. . . .

> Our responsibility is to learn to draw upon the power of the Atonement. Otherwise we walk through mortality relying solely on our own strength. And to do that is to invite the frustration of failure and to refuse the most resplendent gift in time or eternity.[10]

God also sends us help through prophets, family members, friends, and even those on the other side of the veil. This idea is illustrated in the story of Elisha, an Old Testament prophet of the Northern Kingdom of Israel known for his notable miracles. Elisha, also a trusted adviser, counseled the king of Israel on how, where, and when to defend against the Syrians. As Elisha predicted, the king of Syria sent horses and chariots and a great host to surround them. Elisha's servant, overcome with fear, cried to Elisha, "Alas, my master! how shall we do? And he answered, Fear not: for they that be with us are more than they that be with them. And Elisha prayed, and said, Lord, I pray thee, open his eyes, that he may see. And the Lord opened the eyes of the young man; and he saw: and, behold, the mountain was full of horses and chariots of fire round about Elisha" (2 Kings 6:15–17). In reference to Elisha's experience, Elder Jeffrey R. Holland elaborated on this help we receive beyond the veil: "In the gospel of Jesus Christ you have help from both sides of the veil, and you must never forget that. When disappointment and discouragement strike—and they will—you remember and never forget that if our eyes could be opened we would see horses and chariots of fire as far as the eye can see riding at reckless speed to come to our protection. They will always be there, these armies of heaven, in defense of Abraham's seed."[11]

We don't always see who is round about us to calm our fears, strengthen us, and grant us peace. But what we do know is that God sends help, on this side of the veil or on the other. In Doctrine and Covenants 84:88, He tells us, "And whoso receiveth you, there I will be also, for I will go before your face. I will be on your right hand and on your left, and my Spirit shall be in your hearts, and mine angels round about you, to bear you up." This verse has special meaning to me.

Several members of my family have passed away, including my mother, father, sister, brother, mother in-law, father-in-law, and three nephews. Life seems very short to me because I've lost so many people whom I love dearly. But I feel their presence as angels round about me to bear me up. I know we have a loving Heavenly Father who sends angels to comfort and strengthen us. And if we don't have people close to us who have passed away, God sends an army of angels connected to us to bear us up. We may not know them, but they know us! These angels partner with God in ministering to our needs.

God often sends others to walk with us, reminding us that we are not alone, reminding us that we are one family—God's family—and that we can help each other return to Him. Most importantly, He sent His Son to walk the pathway of perfection with us.

Sharing His Help

Calvin, one student in our Camino group, became aware of Christ's willingness to walk with him. He was reminded of Christ's help and the need to share His help. After the first two weeks of walking, Calvin developed severe pain in his lower legs. He was upset with God that his painful legs prevented him from joining the group to walk. He felt betrayed, hurt, and helpless, thinking that God had abandoned him after a spiritual beginning to his experience. Calvin remarked:

> After a few days of not being able to do much more than hobble around, I was in [the village of] O Cebreiro and remembered something that I had seen in Santo Domingo de Silos. There, in the wonderful cloister, is a stone carving of the Savior, dressed in pilgrim clothing, walking with His disciples on the road to Emmaus. I realized that just as Christ had walked with His disciples then, He walked with me now. But this was not all; He also sat with me at the empty bus stops on the days I couldn't walk, and He comforted me when I was in the hospital alone. He never left my side.

Walking on the road to Emmaus, the Savior, dressed in pilgrim clothing, invites all to walk with Him. Photo by John Rosenberg.

> I pondered the Savior's symbol as the Bread of Life. Just as I had eaten bread every day on the Camino, He had accompanied me on my journey. I realized that I began to see His hand in every aspect of my journey, personalized just for me. My companions, other pilgrims, the shopkeepers, they all gave me daily bread. Not just the actual bread that I ate at every meal, but . . . a different kind of bread that fed my soul. They ministered to me and blessed me in ways that only God could have directed.
>
> After rest and a beautiful blessing, I was able to walk again. It was still incredibly painful, but I could feel the Savior by my side. I walked the last 150 km to Santiago, with a new determination to share my daily bread with those around me—not because of some spiritual balance I felt indebted to pay but because of love for my Savior. In the same way that I needed those who fed me, I could feed others on their Camino.
>
> I came to learn that by heeding the Savior's invitation to walk with Him, He will make more of me than I ever hoped to be. Walking with Him means inviting Him to join me and earnestly striving to live as He would by loving and giving freely. He will give me daily bread in the form of people on my path—bread that will sustain me and bread to sustain others. We are all pilgrims—in need of His daily bread.

God also asks us to be His helpers. Elder Marion D. Hanks taught, "Christ will lift us up and help us to become as he is as we do as he did; as we love our Father and give him our lives; as we love each other and all men, and learn and live and teach his word; [and] believe in the worth of souls."[12] To walk with Christ means we accept His help, but it also means we share His help with others. We can become powerful instruments in His hands when those around us experience self-doubt. We can share patience. We can share Christ's love and charity. We can remind others that their honest efforts are enough. We can help others recognize their strengths and affirm that they are children of God with potential to become like Him.

"What does it mean to walk with the Lord?" asked President Henry B. Eyring. "It means to do what He does, to serve the way He serves. He sacrificed His own comforts to bless those in need, so that's what we try to do. . . . If you walk with the Savior long enough, you will learn to see everyone as a child of God with limitless potential, regardless of what his or her past may have been."[13] We are worthy to be instruments in God's hands to represent Him. What an honor He has bestowed upon us! He believes we are capable of loving *for* Him. Can we let Him know that He can count on us to walk the rocky path with others on His behalf? The Savior reminds us, "Ye call me Master and Lord: and ye say well; for so I am. If I then, your Lord and Master, have washed your feet; ye also ought to wash one another's feet. For I have given you an example, that ye should do as I have done to you" (John 13:13–15). *Are we willing to wash one another's feet?* Are we willing to share the love and encouragement of the Lord with those who are in despair, who feel inadequate, who feel they don't measure up, who fear they are not enough, who feel overwhelmed trying to do it all, who doubt who they are and who they may become?

"As ye have therefore received Christ Jesus the Lord, so walk ye in him: rooted and built up in him" (Colossians 2:6–7). Can we love for Him? Can we be an ambassador for Christ in helping others combat self-doubt?

Our Savior from Self-Doubt

Walking the Camino de Santiago in Spain was a powerful experience. We gathered to celebrate the light and life of Jesus Christ—to go "farther and higher" with His help.[14] Our group of students met other pilgrims from Spain, England, Italy, France, Germany, Korea, Israel, Chile, and Peru, to name a few places. People gathered from all over the world to

Opposite: Ascending pebblestone pathway on the Camino de Santiago. Photo by John Rosenberg.

honor Christ, reminding us that we all belong to one another, that we are brothers and sisters in God's eternal family. God gathers His family. The Lord wants us to "be gathered in one, that [we] may be [His] people and [He] will be [our] God" (Doctrine and Covenants 42:9).

All the Camino paths end in Santiago de Compostela, Spain, a city named after the Apostle James. When our students arrived in Santiago, they hugged, cheered, and cried as they gathered to celebrate having completed something truly difficult. What made the journey meaningful to them was the relationships they built as they walked. They realized how much others had helped them along the way, how they had helped others, and how God had helped them. They knew they could not have completed the journey alone.

As we accept Christ's invitation to walk with Him, feelings of self-doubt will transform into feelings of confidence in the Lord. We will overcome feelings of doubt about who we are and what we can become through the love and strength of the Savior. We will think less about ourselves and our weaknesses and more about the will of God and how we can be instruments in His hands to do His work. Focusing on the Savior's help will bring joy and happiness to our journey.

I bear witness that the Savior walks with us. He tells us, "For I the Lord thy God will hold thy right hand, saying unto thee, Fear not; *I will help thee*" (Isaiah 41:13; italics added). He offers to help us when we are impatient with ourselves, and He reminds us of His patience with us. He walks with us when we are critical of and negative about ourselves, reminding us that we are loved and encouraging us to see ourselves through His loving eyes. He walks with us when we fear we are not enough, and He motivates us to try—to offer what we can. He empowers us by making our weak things strong. He grants us special gifts and talents, and He encourages us to recognize and enhance those gifts and talents. He guides us with the Spirit when we feel overwhelmed and helps us prioritize and focus our efforts on doing what is most needful. He reminds us that we are worthy of His help when we make mistakes and when we sin, and He motivates us to change.

When we focus on the Savior, we see evidence of His footsteps beside us, and we recognize the warmth of His patience, charity, power, gifts, voice, and forgiveness. We feel His peace as He calls out, "I am the light of the world: he that followeth me shall not walk in darkness, but shall have the light of life" (John 8:12). We honor Christ as we follow in His footsteps and do as He would do and love as He would love. I know our Savior lives and loves us. I know we will go farther and higher with His help.

I witness of the joy we can find on our personal journey as we stay focused on Christ. Our confidence in who we are and what we may become with Him will wax strong. I know that Jesus Christ *is* our Savior from self-doubt.

Invitation: Focus on the Savior's invitation to become "at-one" with Him and one another. Focus on His gift of unity for you personally and for your family.

Think-in-ink journal challenge: Write down ways you have felt Christ's help in your life. Write one thing you can do today to accept His help more in your life.

Notes

1. See Bible Dictionary, "Hezekiah's Tunnel."
2. "Lead, Kindly Light," *Hymns*, no. 97.
3. Robert D. Hales, "We Can't Do It Alone," *Ensign*, November 1975, 90.
4. Brené Brown, *The Gifts of Imperfection: Let Go of Who You Think You're Supposed to Be and Embrace Who You Are* (Center City, MN: Hazelden, 2010), 20, 74.
5. *Oxford Dictionary of English*, 3rd ed. (2010), s.v. "disable," https://oxfordreference.com/view/10.1093/acref/9780199571123.001.0001/m_en_gb0228820.
6. Hales, "We Can't Do It Alone," 90–91, 93.
7. Jacopo Robusti Tintoretto, *The Washing of the Feet*, 1548–49, oil on canvas, 90 × 210″ (228 × 533 cm), Museo del Prado, Madrid, Spain, https://museodelprado.es/en/the-collection/art-work/the-washing-of-the-feet/77d1fd63-1918-40b7-a79e-6d427e19bed8.
8. Bruce C. Hafen, "Covenant Marriage," *Ensign*, November 1996, 26.
9. Michelle D. Craig, "Divine Discontent," *Ensign*, November 2018, 54.
10. Sheri L. Dew, "Our Only Chance," *Ensign*, May 1999, 66–67.
11. Jeffrey R. Holland, "For Times of Trouble" (Brigham Young University devotional, March 13, 1980), 10, speeches.byu.edu.
12. Marion D. Hanks, *The Gift of Self* (Salt Lake City: Bookcraft, 1974), 262.
13. Henry B. Eyring, "Walk with Me," *Ensign*, May 2017, 84–85.
14. "Dum pater familias" (hymn), lines 19–20, in *Codex Calixtinus*, la.wikisource.org/wiki/codex_calixtinus/dum_pater_familias.

INDEX

F

G

H

K

L

M

N

O

U

V

W

Y